45 DAYS
TO HIRED

ERIN D. HUGHES
WITH JOHN WALKER

Dedication

To my mother, a 5-foot 2-inch hero, who told a goliath of a woman, "He will not dig ditches!" and to her sister, who has helped me remember the power of family.

A Notice for Print Readers

I had initially intended this to be for sale as an eBook only. After review of the material I felt it could be significantly more effective in print form.

Throughout the book there are images, diagrams, and URL's that do not expand well. To see these in full color and resolution go to https://45daystohired.com/resouces In the Resources section you will be able to download the Master List as well as the Workflow diagrams and Cover Letter and Resume examples.

https://45daystohired.com/about The About page has an expanded list of References from page 175 that allows you to click through and read, watch, and listen to them.

All resources are provided at zero cost. You do need to check them out as part of a shopping cart workflow but there is no charge for the original content provided in the book.

Finally check https://45daystohired.com/ for updates and additional content that will be coming soon.

TABLE OF CONTENTS

INTRODUCTION

Just about any time in my life, but mostly in school and even more so in third grade, especially, I just did not fit in. I tried; I really did, but schoolwork just did not work for me. I wanted to have fun and play and do interesting and creative things.

I was raised in a small town in upstate New York, just south of Buffalo, during the 70s and 80s. I had been having trouble in school ever since day one. My teachers struggled to control me and stop the insistent sea of *"why's"* and *"and why do I have to…. "*

In third grade, I literally could not do anything right. One day I managed to sneak into school with a tank top that said, "Super Star."

It was February. In upstate New York.

This was unacceptable.

The teacher sent me to the hall. The principal came and clamped his hand down on my neck and reinforced exactly how unacceptable. I got it... no tank tops, and certainly no running around the classroom flexing my little pipe cleaner arms yelling, "I'm a Super Star!"

That night I told my parents what had happened. This set off a shit storm of parent-teacher meetings.

My mom and dad went into my classroom after school with my teacher and the principal, a few days later. The next time I saw them in the hallway outside my classroom, my mother, all 80 lbs. at 5'2" was yelling straight up at a giant 6'2" monster of a woman who was my 3rd-grade teacher *"He will not dig ditches!"* and my father holding the principal, who was a good 6 inches taller than him, up against the wall with a fist full of his shirt and tie in one hand and with his other fist clenched by his side.

I did not dig ditches. I dug fox holes, filled sandbags, walked long, hard walks and carried heavy packs. I learned to lead from the best and eventually grew as a leader to become a Sergeant of Marines.

My leadership grew, but the pain and process of learning to become a leader did not stop after I separated from the Marine Corps, became interested in computers, or moved to Japan, or any of the other trials I faced along the way. I always knew I wanted more, to be better, to be a success, far beyond what a 3rd-grade teacher would tell me.

Today I trade my time for money and utilize my experiences and ability to boil down complex product jargon into technology outcomes for customers.

No matter who tells you, "You are not good enough," or not strong enough, not smart enough. They are judging you at a specific time and place, against a perceived notion they are biased too. They are also discounting the person you can grow to be.

However, you can only grow to be that person if you decide to.

The only question is, will YOU decide to become that person?

Thank You

I know this book can help you find your way out of job seeking peril, so thank you for buying the book.

I would like to thank my mother and father, my brother, sister, wife, kids and family. My list of mentors who have helped and encouraged me throughout the trials and tribulations are listed in the Mentors, Family and Friends. Mentors who, now when I speak to others, hear their words coming out of my mouth.

If you are desperate to get right to it, please skip to Section 3 where we talk about executing a process that will get you interviews and measure the results.

However, after a couple of attempts, you will want to come back to the first two sections to review the basics.

Section 1

DEALING with Fate

"Fate is like a strange, unpopular restaurant filled with odd little waiters who bring you things you never asked for and don't always like."

Lemony Snick

That's going to leave a mark....

I was called into the office; I knew what was coming.

For the past 5 and a half years, I had been a leader in my company. I had come to the company as an individual contributor and rose to manager. I had led several teams and that seemed my niche, a new business problem that needed someone to build a team or an old team floundering under poor leadership.

A year ago, things changed. Adding a new CIO who I now reported directly to and blundered my first couple of interactions with, until I got onto his cadence. Unfortunately, by then, he had decided to replace me.

All my initiatives for the next year except the most necessary ones were shelved. I recognized our styles were at odds and made numerous attempts to bridge the gap and work with the CIO. I welcomed a fresh set of eyes. Ok, I accepted a fresh set of eyes on our issues and was willing and able to work to help solve them. Instead, I found my sphere of influence shrinking and my ability to maneuver within the company's landscape diminish.

When I was moved to manage our security team, I knew it was not a good fit. I had a minimal amount knowledge running a security team. I gradually slipped from an ultra-motivated leader to a nuisance. I was not ready to change jobs and was not ready to give up the good fight for a mission and company I believed in.

The day before, there had been problems. The decisions I had made or failed to make had left a project in the hands of a less competent team and caused a 10-minute outage of one of our services. I took the blame for not managing the transition of those issues correctly.

Two choices were placed on the desk in front of me, one a separation package, the other a Personal Improvement Plan (PIP). My boss explained I would not survive the PIP.

I walked out the door for the last time. I was devastated but smiled and laughed like it was nothing. Immediately my phone rang and beeped with calls and texts from concerned co-workers. I assured everyone I would be fine, but really, I did not know.

I went home at my regular time, too embarrassed to tell my wife what had happened. I did not have my company computer and could only rely on my son's PC.

I sat in front of it that night and stared at the screen drinking a beer and saying, "Man, I could do that, then start to apply and say "augh ..." till I fell asleep at the computer desk.

Accountability and Responsibility

Some basic math.

If you earned $3000 a month before you lost your job, and you received a "package" when you left that was basically your existing Paid Time Off for 1 month. You have $4500 in the bank in cash. Your mortgage is $1000. Your car payment is $300. Your utilities are $400 this time of year. Your groceries $400 a month, your gas and other miscellaneous expenses are $400-500. Finally, do not forget about the credit card you finance all the things you cannot afford, another $500 a month. With these figures, how long can you go without a job?

Do you suck at word problems? Good, so do I. I made this helpful little table.

The Crisis Calculator		
Liabilities	Payments	Balance
Current Balance		$4500
Package	$3000	$7500
Mortgage/Rent	$1000	$6500
Car Payment	$300	$6200
Utilities	$400	$5800
Groceries	$400	$5400
Other Miscellaneous Expenses	$300	$5100
Credit Card	$500	$4600
End Month 1		$4600
Mortgage/Rent	1000	$3600

Car Payment	$300	$3300
Utilities	$400	$2900
Groceries	$400	$2500
Other Miscellaneous Expenses	$300	$2200
Credit Card	$500	$1700
End Month 2		$1700
Mortgage/Rent	$1000	$700
Car Payment	$300	$400
Utilities	$400	$0.00
Groceries	$400	$400.00
Other Miscellaneous Expenses	$300	$700.00
Credit Card	$500	$1200.00
End Month 3		1200.00

You see that in the first month, you are ok, the next, you are digging into your savings, and finally, in month 3 you are using your credit cards to finance everything.

This seems like simple math for those who do not save, or others who cannot make sense of the twists and turns of life. I attempted to keep the numbers easy to demonstrate a simple point; you are responsible for your family and providing for them.

You may have a spouse or significant other who can help carry the weight while you figure out your next steps, but I did not have that luxury. I was the single source of income for our family. It was up to me.

Contacts Companies and Positions

When I woke the next morning, my wife had gone out of town early to deal with family issues and getting our three children off to school, with packed lunches and the correct clothes was up to me. I did not have a plan in place to deal with this and struggled. I pushed through the situation and none of the children were late. No one went to school looking ridiculous, and all had a packed form of food I had made. They would not starve, look dumb or arrive late.

Pretty successful start to my first day of unemployment!

Then reality hit again… I DO NOT HAVE A JOB!

How was I going to do this? I needed to figure out my situation quickly and get on it.

I thought about some recruiters from my past. They could not move fast enough, never seemed to have relevant openings, and they were more closely aligned with the client's needs than mine.

No recruiters.

I checked my phone and another slew of text messages and 2 or 3 voicemails. When I counted it all up, there were over 50 people who offered help and connections.

You ever have one of those days where you are drowning in work and think you do not have a second to breathe, let alone help someone else, but you stop and help that one coworker with a problem because you know it is the quickest route to resolution for them?

I do. The day after you have lost your job and you get text messages from people who "can't believe it…" or are "shocked, what were they thinking?" and ends with a "let me know if you need anything" or "my friend might be able to help."

That is why you did it.

I made a list of people with the influence and ability to help. Then I looked at their connections on LinkedIn and found another 20 people I had known over the years.

Boom… instant progress. I now had a list of almost 70 names.

With those names, I had the CONTACTS!

I also had a list of names with affiliations with the companies that could make introductions. This factor alone bolstered my resolve this was not impossible. I was connecting dots that would lead me to other people or companies that could help me out of my situation.

After combing through lists of Contacts, I found the second piece of the puzzle, COMPANIES.

In the next two days, I sent out 71 emails, some with resumes.

Some of those resumes highly customized, others just a one size fits all general overviews to see if there was any interest. Over the next three weeks, those resumes and cover letters, along with follow-up emails and revised resumes, turned into 28 phone calls, that led to about 20 real phone interviews, that turned into about 12-second phone interviews to another 3 in-person interviews and finally to 2 more in-person interviews with both ending in employment offers.

The initial batch of resumes I sent out to Contacts and Companies comprised 56 of those emails. The rest were complete blind shots in the dark.

Of the blind shots in the dark, one brief semi-interested corporate recruiter who did not understand the questions he was asking or the answers he was supposed to get led nowhere. For those 20 attempts, I was competing on Position.

The blind shots in the dark where Contacts and Companies are unknown, I call Position. Applying on Position is the least likely to net you any success, which is why we will look at it last.

All the tools in this book are built around a few core concepts.

- **Mindset** There is no way to stress this enough. **You must** wake up every morning, ready to face one million defeats in search of one victory.

- **Contacts** People you have worked with previously or done business with who know you and can be asked to vouch for you.

- **Companies** These can be competing companies in your space or supporting companies that help fulfill a mission to create a product or service.

- **Positions** These are positions you are qualified for and think you can get in a reasonably short while.

- **Tools** Utilizing the correct tools for your job search will help you understand what needs work and what is getting traction.

- **Workflow** How you will utilize all the above tools and techniques to gain access to the people who can employ you. Work the system, to make it work for you.

- With the two offers I received, I took the one that seemed to be the best fit, not the highest dollar amount. I needed stability, and the person who referred me internally was a friend and I wanted to see her profit from recommending me.

Time to target. Just under five weeks. I made it and was now gainfully employed in 43 working days.

SECTION 2

MINDSET, TOOLS & RESOURCES

"We shape our tools and afterwards our tools shape us."

Marshall McLuhan

Mindset

First, we need to talk about a basic understanding of our goal. Mindset. Our mission statement will deliver purpose into what we are trying to accomplish.

"To find a new position that will allow me to provide for my family at or near our current lifestyle."

What does this statement say? "GET A F#$KING JOB!"

What does this statement NOT SAY?

- "Make $20k more than my previous position."

- "Work on X technology instead of Y technology."

- "Never have to listen to a boss I hate again."

- "Never have to stand in line again."

- "Become the Vice President of Marketing at XYX Corp."

All the things on the above list can happen for you. For each of these goal statements, I know a job candidate who has achieved each one in their job search. But guess what? These moves came not from an emergency get a F#$KING job crisis. Instead, they resulted from calculated career planning from candidates who have cultivated reputations as reliable, intelligent hard workers. They are known as people who can be relied on for their judgment and integrity. We are not talking about this type of career planning.

We are talking about jumpstarting your revenue stream that has suddenly stopped.

If your financial situation was a hospital patient, it would be on life support; you need to get it breathing again, make sure the heart is pumping and then stop the bleeding. This is not the time for making aspirations about what you want from your career. Steady the ship, get new funds coming in. For right now, get off life support, then we will work on running the marathon.

I will remind you of this mindset repeatedly throughout the book. This is not meant to sap your confidence. Remember, someone hired you in the first place, so you are a competent doer. What I want, though, are reminders to keep a tight laser focus on the goal that finding gainful employment in 45 days, or less. Reminding you that your revenue stream is ZERO, and you are the person in charge of making that change.

Since YOU are the person in charge of making that happen, you need to do a few things.

- Remove excuses. You have no one else to blame but yourself. Sure, "*so and so did not do like you told them to…*" or "*This and that product did not sell as well as it should have.*" It doesn't matter.

    - Motivate you to act. You can rely on Unemployment Insurance or some other subsidies. That might get you by, but is it going to help you look your kids in the face and tell them you put food on the table?

- Develop a winning mindset. If you keep saying, "I can fix this," "what is my next step," "how can I win this" I guarantee you will start to see the answers and move in a positive direction.

- Here is a great video I like to watch to help with my mindset. Winners Win

Daily Routine

A few years back, I had an acquaintance who I had recommended for a position within my company I was hiring for. Believe it or not, this technically competent system administrator who I had vouched for arrived at my office for the interview wearing a short sleeve button-down with the top 3 buttons unbuttoned, revealing his sweat-soaked t-shirt beneath. Do not be that guy or gal.

Right now, you are probably sitting home, working on new resumes, and sending out emails trying to get some traction. You may NOT be showering daily or putting on clean clothes and trying to look your best. YOU SHOULD BE!

- Always look presentable, a video call or a chance to meet someone face to face might pop up, and it is one less thing to be stressed about.

- Wake up on time and put diligence into your day and your appearance.
- Plan your day, have some daily practices that help you stay focused and on track.
- Shower every day and follow a similar routine to when you had a job. Wake up early. **Your new job is finding a job.**
- You will have some downtime, study articles and books related to your field. Work on a new or in-demand certification.
- Read some fiction. As few as 10 to 20 pages a day will do the trick. Use it to give your mind a rest from all the "Work-Related" reading and writing you should be doing. I like to spend at least one hour with my kids' reading together and then discussing what we read. This is a great way to open lines of communication and spend time together while taking the focus away from your other problems.
- Write a blog post on your field and post it somewhere. LinkedIn and other career sites are always looking for content and if you have something interesting and informative to say, it will only help you in your job search having a good reference for your skills.
- I cannot stress this enough, EXERCISE! Remember when you said you wish you had the time to exercise? Now you do, GET SOME!

- Get out of your house. Call old colleagues up, offer coffee or lunch to talk about the market or other subjects that will help keep you current. Remember that you are on a budget, so throw out a subtle mention you are looking for work. Most people will be happy to pay or at least split the bill to help you out.
- Contact others in your network and look for help from them to introduce you to potential employers.

Notebook and a Pen

I never looked at this as a must-have until a friend named Michael talked about how he did not select a candidate because he did not bring a notebook with him to the interview. This was a sales job and in situations where you are meeting with someone to talk about a sale or a job, your memory is not infallible, so taking notes is a must.

- Buy a brand-new notebook to take notes in. The habit of writing things down increases your memory and cognition, as well as helps provide valuable information for later.
- Amazon offers a 5X7 Amazon brand notebook with grid lines instead of plain lines. The grid lines are helpful for sketching ideas and diagrams out in a pinch.

- As the interviewers are talking, take notes, these are handy for later to craft succinct follow-ups.

Entrepreneurship

There is nothing wrong with becoming an entrepreneur. NOTHING! Successful entrepreneurs create more options and have the potential to make unscalable truckloads of money.

Before you take the leap, though, there is no easy way to tell you this gently and it must be said. If you did not have the discipline to commit to the 9-5 of the job you previously held, would you have the discipline to execute on a plan that will hold only a vague hope of paying off sometime in the future? Possibly the very distant future, if ever?

If your answer is YES, you are reading the wrong book. The 4-hour Work Week is in its 2nd revision, buy that.

This book is about reality.

This book is about putting money in the bank every two weeks, keeping food on the table, a roof over your head and hopefully having a few beers in the fridge. Now that we have a clear goal let us find some tools to execute on that goal.

If you choose not to heed this advice and instead want to jump into the entrepreneurship pool with both feet fine, I am glad to be proven wrong. But one last bit of advice, keep your "conventional" LinkedIn profile and career search as a back-up. Do not remove the consistency of your LinkedIn profile with flashy updates showcasing your newfound aspirations and looking like you have just joined the cult of get rich quick.

Instead, start a second LinkedIn account and a personal page that gives you the background to match that aspiration, also start a company profile that fits the niche or services you wish to provide. Work on your 4 Hour Work Week plan in parallel or after hours, but whatever you do, stay on course with finding a new position.

TOOLS

Finding new employment is about utilizing a combination of your Skills, Experiences and Contacts to put you in a new position. Encompassing all of that is the tools you will use to communicate effectively and accurately and then measure the results of your attempts at communication to understand what you can do better.

The tool set we will use gives us a starting point then helps us out by providing us resources that can be drawn upon to ensure that what we are doing is taking us in the correct direction.

- Google Apps & Email address
- LinkedIn
- Your Resume
- Your Cover Letter/Introduction Email
- Resume.com
- Yesware
- JobScan.co
- Hunter.io
- Toastmasters
- Social Media Do's and Don'ts (Mostly Don'ts)
- On Lying

Success largely depends on doing the right basics repeatedly. The first couple of emails I put out in that 2-day span were… ugly, but by the time I got down to the last 30, the format was tight, the message was clear, and I was gaining more traction with every communication. Here is a list of the basic do's and don'ts before we get started. I should not have to iterate these, but just in case... I am doing it anyway.

Google Apps

If you do not have a Google account for whatever reason, get a Google mail account BUT SEE #2 FIRST, unless you are already in the Microsoft camp and have a O365 account with all of the bells and whistles.

I have domains hosted on Google Apps for almost ten years now. I store my project data, resumes, and other initiatives I am working in this one location. Google Apps is available from any device with an internet connection and a web browser, making it convenient to download a copy of your latest resume and then send it to a new contact, while waiting in line at Walmart, the dentist's office or from your phone or anywhere.

To add a technical flair and a bit of personality to your email, purchase your domain and point the MX record to Google. The cost is about $100 a year and demonstrates a technical understanding of concepts like DNS that, in an IT technical interview, give you a leg up, even though it is super easy, and anyone can set it up.

In 2020 you can get an Office 365 family account for around a hundred dollars and get all the pro-tools needed like Word, PowerPoint and Excel. These are great options, but the Google account is free and comes with all the apps you need to assist you in your job search.

Also, Google Apps has add-ons like DocHub, which allows you to edit and sign PDF files and Yesware that allows you to track sent emails, come built-in and follow your account anywhere you sign in.

Email

Every email address matters. In the late 90s, I had business cards made with my email address huge6669@yahoo.com after a funny song from the band Coven I had heard. No one got the joke, and no one emailed me. Ever.

If your name is Jack Samuel Smith, then think up something clever, but like jacksamsmith or jack.sam.smith or js.smith329, the possibilities are endless. Just keep it PC.

[EXAMPLES]	Scores
jsmsmith@gmail.com	GOOD
jackloveskittys@gmail.com	BAD
jackateyourgoldfish@gmail.com	Just Do Not

Jackateyourgoldfish is reminiscent of your fraternity or military days, catchy, funny but probably not a career driver as far as emails to respond to.

WAIT! "All my friends know my email as Jackateyourgoldfish@gmail.com!!"

Your friends who are adults will understand the change, and it is 2020, you can have more than one email address. Just make sure the most professional sounding one is the one you are putting on your resume and is linked to your LinkedIn account and any other accounts you need like Indeed or Glassdoor.

Finally, understand that you can change your account settings, to reflect your name or any other information you would like. I go with just my first and last name, but you can also add titles or prefixes. At the end of your name clarifiers like JR 1st, 2nd, 3rd.

To do this go to Gmail in your web browser > Settings (Gear Icon) > See all Settings > Accounts > Send mail as > edit info.

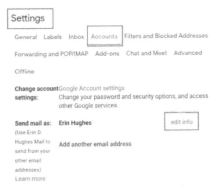

LINKEDIN

After sorting out your email, LinkedIn is our next must-use tool. If you do not have a LinkedIn account, no problem, sign-up now and create one. It is free to network if you do not choose the premium account. This is social networking for professionals that helps you connect with people who can aid you in your job search and you can give back and help them. If you already have an account, great feel free to skip this section, but if you think your profile could use a tune-up or if you're not familiar with LinkedIn at all, in the next few sections will walk through the platform together to help you make sure your profile is up to date.

We will also talk about utilizing the platform to alert you of new jobs, cultivate contacts, see hiring trends in companies, and grow your network.

Returning to our mindset discussion, remember to select positions and titles you are qualified for. Not your dream position. We are looking to get our income source back. That is it.

LinkedIn is important. Almost as important as the resume you are sending to potential hiring managers. It is where anyone in the world can see what you say your skills are and how you articulate them.

I call LinkedIn "your resume in long form." This is where you get down to brass tacks and fill out everything you ever did and how you did it—reviewing our profile with a new critical eye to weaknesses that could allow potential employers to discount us as a serious candidate. At the end of this chapter, I will show you two cool tips you can use to make your long-form resume stand out above everyone else.

Let us go through your LinkedIn profile section by section and explain what it is and why you should be putting time into making it look polished.

Your Picture

A picture is worth 1000 words.

A Picture is a MUST, a simple, good-looking headshot.

The photo does not need to be a professional suit and tie shot. I had the same LinkedIn profile picture for years. A co-worker took this one, she said I needed to smile, told me a joke, and snapped the pic on her iPhone.

A good rule of thumb is, "If I posted this as my Facebook profile photo, would people think I am boring? If yes, that is the shot you want." Other tips include Make sure your photo is of you, you take up 60% of the frame, be the only person in the picture and avoid confusing or distracting backgrounds.

No weird poses like planking in a crowded elevator or any other goofy stuff like that. Just a picture of you, and your shining, smiling face.

I have almost 1000 connections on LinkedIn of people who take their public image and positions seriously. Of those at last count, only four did not have profile pictures.

About

Crisp clean and to the point. Remember, this is the long form of your resume, so you can list a few accomplishments but also keep it concise and a bit exciting.

Below are a couple of good examples of objective statements.

This objective statement by my friend Gina, who is an incredible Project Manager but also has a very persuasive personality and can work across different business units to achieve winning outcomes for any company.

Successfully delivering projects at various stages for over 15 years with extensive background in managing Waterfall, Agile, and hybrid projects. Proven leader in enhancing cross-team collaborations and processes. Results driven. Recognized for developing improved organizational change management procedures and communication paths, skilled in team development, executive coaching, SDLC, and service delivery.

I like Gina's objective, and its directness. She uses action words like, proven, extensive, and recognized. There are no wasted words. Gina does not use "I" or "Me" or "I am", because the conversation is all about her abilities and what she can do for your company.

This one was mine for a long time, it was easy to craft and I think it says volumes about what I am capable of.

An experienced leader seeking new opportunities, capable of working easily in fast-paced, challenging technological organizations that value ease of use and reliability. Strengths include the ability to architect solutions and create clear, executive-level communications on engineering and IT operations while executing approved plans with discipline and transparency.

When not in the job market, I simply remove "seeking new opportunities."

Here are some not so good examples. I wish I had made some of these up, but sadly I found them on LinkedIn for everyone to see.

An experienced leader who knows how to handle things looking for work.

A ready, willing and able system administrator looking for work.

Part-time entrepreneur seeking drilling work.

Welcoming and involved CEO seeks new position in Houston with a high 6 figure salary, telecommuting and company paid apartment required.

You are trying to sell yourself as capable and intelligent. The About section is like your objective statement on your resume. You need to be self-aware of your strengths and make them interesting to potential employers. Without self-assessment and an eye on the market, you may not be able to position yourself properly and intelligently explain your value to someone else. On LinkedIn, where we showcase your resume in long form, expand past one simple sentence.

Background/Experience

This is where you get granular with the facts and details of what you did. Think problem statement, think resolution. I could honestly use a bit more of that on my own statements, but we can work on that together.

Looking at two of my background statements, we can experiment and see if we can make them better. I do not honestly remember where I heard of the below technique to describe your positions, but I love it, I use it, and I look for it in other's resumes.

The best way to describe your role is 3-fold.

- **What was the problem?**
- **What did you do?**
- **What was the outcome?**

Using some of my background statements as a crash test dummy.

I am an AWS Solutions Architect. After passing the exam, though, I rarely worked in an AWS production environment. One day I was looking at some of the documentation and found it sloppy and unstructured. I rewrote it, and that led to becoming the AWS Subject Matter Expert, and eventually building that into an entire piece of our practice with process and workflows that support, and other organizations utilize. All from just being willing to take over a little bit of documentation.

The first time I thought about putting that on my resume, I wrote the following.

Create, implement, and document new process procedures and tools around the deployment of AWS and Azure security products.

Now considering what the problem was, and how it was affecting us, and how we solved it, I have this now on LinkedIn.

Recognized a deficiency in documentation, process, and procedures, for solutions in AWS and Azure. Created documents, and workflows, while working across organizations to train and educate other business units on the proper procedures, resulting in better business continuity and customer experience in cloud onboardings.

They both say the same thing pretty much. The difference is how they say it. In the second example, there is a clear call to action, *"Recognized a deficiency in documentation, process, procedures and tools for solutions in AWS and Azure"* That shows a clear problem, it shows what I built to fix the problem *"created documents, and workflows"* and what I did for parts of the problem that were out of my control *"while working across organizations to train and educate other business units on the proper procedures and contacts."* Finally, the outcome which was *"better business continuity and customer experience in cloud onboardings."*

This next example is from my first IT job ever. One day, my old salty former Marine boss was gone, the next day, this little Italian ball of intensity took his place. The company had purchased another company that needed access to our management tools. I had a Microsoft Certified Professional Certification. That was all my formal training at the time.

I came to work and there was a stack of Cisco Routers and software box that said Citrix MetaFrame on it and a note that said, "See me when you get in" -Jim.

Jim or "Bubby" as I called him because he called everyone "Bubby," explained that I needed to connect all the remote offices through ATM/Frame Relay with the Cisco routers, and then share our CRM application Commerce at Work, with all the remote offices. Oh yeah and they all need to use our Exchange 5.5 email server. Fortunately, I could make a hardware purchase of one server, $1000. This was 1999, no Google, no real online forums, or places with rich tech advice.

This story could go on for hours with twists, turns, OS requirements and hardware misunderstandings and storage problems. What happened?

I called support for Commerce at Work and Citrix, both told me, *"We don't support that."* When I tried to explain it to Bubby, he just looked at me, tapped his watch with his forefinger and said, *"Clocks ticking, September 1 is coming!"*

I figured out how to use Citrix. I figured out how to make the routers talk to each other. How to keep a NT4 domain controller with Exchange 5.5 chugging, even with a RAID 5 array of 3, 9GB SCSI disks. I figured out how to share the Commerce at Work Application with Citrix.

In the end, I got it done under budget and on time. The solution was not the most elegant, but it worked. Commerce at Work & Citrix sent Engineers to "advise me on best practices" but really to see how I had architected the solution.

Why would someone need to know all these details?

This **very defining** thing, in the formative stages of my IT career in a couple of lines and how do I make it RELEVANT 20 years later?

All calls I have had with questions about my resume, my life in technology, only roughly 7 of those calls ever make it back that far to my first IT job. Having just enough to entice them to ask about it, regardless if they were from Rochester, or they used Cisco with ATM or Exchange 5.5 before it was uncool, it was a hook, that kept interest in me as a person. A person who could fill a need for the interviewer. In 2015 without a job and looking to sharpen my resume. I reduced my job description from these two bullet points to one.

Two Bullet Points

- Created a multi-location WAN utilizing Citrix Meta-Frame 1.8 over frame relay, Cisco 1720 routers, and Microsoft Windows 2000 server and NT 4.0 client products to achieve utilization of a single user application over the WAN.

- Administered an MS Exchange 5.5 server for a multi-location domain, improving security, reliability, and performance.

- Condensing them to one
- Acquisition and mergers created a situation where the need to work from a single source of truth in distribution was a business driver. With availability and accountability as a driving factor, we created a multi-location WAN utilizing Citrix Meta-Frame 1.8 over frame relay, Cisco routers, and Microsoft Windows 2000 server in NT4 and Exchange 5.5 environment to push production forward.

Education

Should be a no-brainer for most individuals, but there are some exceptions. First, if you have education from somewhere and you have the paper to prove it, list it under Education. If you do not have or have not completed any higher-level education, that is ok, neither did I; you can still get a good job with a great salary. If you are thinking, "*Fake, it till you make it,*" do not do it. Lying makes the hiring process more stressful and less certain. See the section titled On Lying at the end of this section.

License and Certificates

Again, remember this is the long-form of your resume, so every cert you ever received is fair game here. Even put the expired ones if you feel they are still relevant to the type of positions you are going for.

Volunteer Experience

About six years ago, my friend John from the Marines called. He had exciting news. His grandfather's Silver Star medal for combat valor had been retroactively upgraded to the Congressional Medal of Honor for his sacrifice to the country during the Korean War by then-President Obama. John and I reunited with our old Platoon Sergeant and developed a plan to honor his Grandfather, Sergeant Major Michael C. Pena, by walking 64 miles in the blazing hot Texas sun. One mile for every year, he and his family waited to get the award.

We raised about $5,300.00 to establish a college scholarship in his memory and raised awareness in the community that three of the Medal of Honor recipients from the State of Texas had originated in Wharton County, Texas.

People appreciate when others give back to the community and by showing you can work well with others, when you're not getting paid to do it, this is typically an excellent sign to recruiting managers you are not a jerk.

An IMPORTANT note, two years ago, LinkedIn changed their notifications for Volunteer Experience, so adding more volunteer experience does not notify the people in your network of the change. Still, it is high on my list of things I check for in potential employees.

I also coached my son's rugby team for about six years. I loved it and loved the closeness it brought between my son and me. More importantly, it showed I was able to work with a team, coach, and mentor them and get them to the highest level possible.

Finally, it provided small talk and ice breakers between the interviewers and me with similar experiences.

Skills & Endorsements

Here is where you need help from friends to have them endorse you. Remember that you can have only 50 skills you can be endorsed for, and you can pin your top 3 you would like to be recognized for by clicking on the Edit pencil in the Skills & Endorsements section.

RECOMMENDATIONS

RECOMMENDATIONS It is in all caps… because it is important. Remember all those people who called and texted you saying they wanted to help? Here is a quick, easy way for them to help and for future employers to see you are really a great employee.

Contact those people who you said they would love to help you and get them to give you feedback on your resume, LinkedIn profile and ask them to write you a recommendation. Most people, even close friends, will be a little skeptical, but it is a necessary part of your long-form resume.

While everyone is different, when assessing a potential new hire on LinkedIn, I go directly for recommendations. Then if I like what I see there, I move back up to their background and experience.

I make it a practice to ask 2 to 5 of my co-workers when I am preparing to exit the company to write me a review. This can be hard to do, but necessary. Talk to people you worked with directly, and others who know you and your work ethic in the company.

The recommendation process allows you to vet what others say about you before publishing their comments. You can ask for corrections, or clarity, if something needs changing. Finally, you can add or remove the recommendations if needed.

Accomplishments

List out awards or any other thing that does not neatly fit into the other boxes. Here is where I talk about my passion for rugby and coaching boys to become men. Professional organizations you are a part of should be listed here and go into a little detail about your duties there.

Supported Languages

If you speak more than one language, here is the place to make it know. This spot also gives you the ability to show your fluency. So, if you can simply speak Japanese or you can read it and write it, it allows for that type of granularity.

There is what you need on LinkedIn. Get in there and make it happen. This portion of the work should take you about eight hours. If you already have a LinkedIn profile and it just needs some updates, maybe four, but you must get in and do the work, so the rest of the internet can see why they should hire you.

Stand Outs

Two potential areas that can help you stand out on LinkedIn.

The first and most important is your LinkedIn URL. You can customize the URL people see when they go to your profile. This is useful for your signature line on your personal email and lets someone click a link and go directly to your LinkedIn profile.

To edit this, go to your profile and click the Edit button on the top right in your profile section > in the dialog box that appears. Scroll down to contact info and click the pencil icon. Next to that > at the very top, you will see profile URL. Edit that to give you a great link! This can be anything like your name or something you are known for. See the examples below for ideas.

The second is more subjective but choose a good-looking photo that is something that inspires you and add that to the top of your LinkedIn profile. It can be anything you want, but something that reflects your core values and beliefs is a great idea.

I lived in Japan for a couple of years in a town called Gotemba, which had picturesque views of Mount Fuji. This photo was taken just after sunset, one cool winter evening.

To edit this, go to your profile and click the Edit button on the top right in your profile section, > in the dialog box that appears, select the pencil icon next to the default picture.

Click save when you are done with your profile and you will have your new profile header image and URL.

My results are below. Notice the URL, neat and clean and looks great in a signature block!

This is what it looks like in your Signature Block. Simple and clean with all the contact info anyone could need right there.

--

Erin D. Hughes
Phone:555-555-8555
https://www.linkedin.com/in/erindhughes/

Here is an example from my friend Mathew. "Run to Trouble" was a motto he had, and it exemplifies his attitude perfectly. Also, notice how his background picture shows he is a bit of a fun goofball to work with.

GENERATE INFORMATION FROM LINKEDIN

Let's talk about what LinkedIn can do for you to help you see more positions that are open in areas you would like to work in.

LinkedIn can help you articulate that you are looking for work beyond your objective statement. To start, go to your profile and click on the box that says "Show recruiters you are open to work – you control who sees this"

The dialog box will appear.

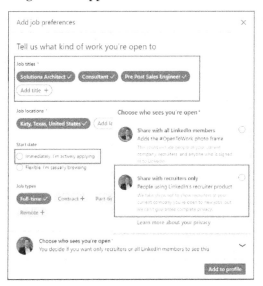

- You can select 1 – 5 Job Titles, search the titles available till you come up with 3-5 that you are clearly qualified for based on your skills and experience.
- Choose your Job locations: These fields will only be filled by locations in the system. You can choose up to 5.
- Start date: Choose Immediately or Flexible. I always toggle on Immediately.
- Job Types: I always check Full-time and Remote. If you are open to Contract, Part Time, Internship or Temporary, select them. I find the Contract option will fill your inbox with a lot of garbage, so I do not recommend it.
- Finally, choose who sees you are open. I always select **"Share with recruiters only"**.
- There is a new #OpenToWork hashtag and photo frame currently available. I think it looks trashy and desperate, but if you want to really reach the broadest market possible, you can turn it on. Besides the aesthetics of the photo, I also do not find real value in saying you have been laid off, fired or whatever from your former position. Your friends and contacts will know your situation. Those should be the first group you are reaching out to. This feature has not been around long enough to judge its effectiveness. Still, it will likely just fill your inbox with SPAM from recruiters looking to fill

positions, not in your geographical area, not inside your industry or outside your skill or knowledge level.

Job Alerts

LinkedIn offers Job Searches and Alerts sent directly to your inbox. This is a time-saving feature you can utilize so you do not bog yourself down in the interface doing specific searches repeatedly.

To receive these Job Alerts. On LinkedIn, select the Jobs Icon and fill in the Job Title you are looking for and the location. I hate morning drives in Houston, so I always choose Remote. Your type of job may not allow for that so fill in your city and state if applicable.

From here, you can get super granular about what you want to receive in your notifications and how. These selections are available from left to right on my interface.

- Relevance -- Most relevant/Most recent
- Timing – This gives you posts from specific time frames Past 24 hours/Past Week/Past Month/Any Time.
- Experience Level – Choose the one relevant to your experience level Internship/Entry Level/Associate/Mid-Senior level/Director/Executive
- LinkedIn Features – Choose 1 or 2 that apply to your situation Easy Apply/Under 10

Applicants/In Your Network/Fair Chance Employer

- All Filters – This gives you the ability to choose more filters like Company/Industry/Job Function/Experience Level/Location/Title/Benefits I would keep as many options open initially. As you get used to the results being provided, you can select more specifics you think you would be qualified for.
- When satisfied with the selections you have made, toggle on the Job Alerts and configure the frequency. For the first week, select daily, then when you have an initial set of results, you can change the frequency to weekly.
- See the below screenshots for details if you cannot find some of the options covered.

Jobs Search

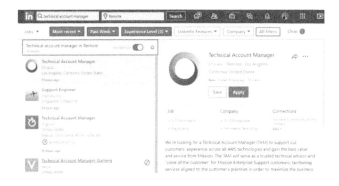

All Filters

Create search alert

This is the first step to getting actionable intelligence delivered to your inbox to aid you in your job search. You can set up multiple job searches for multiple positions and locations if you like. Remember to keep them relevant to your skills and past positions.

LinkedIn Premium

LinkedIn – Premium Subscription -- DISCLAIMER -- I am not affiliated in any way with LinkedIn.

I recommend the premium subscription. Remember that the goal of this job search is to be employed in 45 days. LinkedIn gives you a free 30 days, which means you should only need to pay for one month. There is a wealth of knowledge to be gained in that 30 days, and last I checked, it was only 30$ a month.

Why? LinkedIn Premium Careers gives you the following.

- 3 InMail credits a month to recruiters
- Shows everyone who has viewed your profile
- Shows you as a featured applicant
- Provides application insights

I know we said we will not use recruiters, but you can InMail them with Premium if you need to.

Seeing who has viewed your profile and how you stacked up against the competition are especially useful. Look at a screenshot here and the wealth of information provided by LinkedIn Premium.

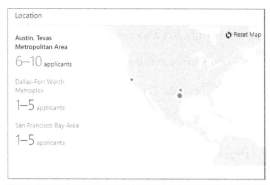

Location

**Austin, Texas
Metropolitan Area**

6—10 applicants

Dallas-Fort Worth
Metroplex

1—5 applicants

San Francisco Bay Area

1—5 applicants

↻ Reset Map

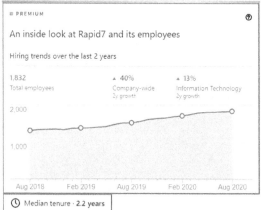

▦ PREMIUM   ⑦

An inside look at Rapid7 and its employees

Hiring trends over the last 2 years

1,832   ▲ 40%   ▲ 13%
Total employees   Company-wide   Information Technology
                         2y growth   2y growth

2,000

1,000

Aug 2018   Feb 2019   Aug 2019   Feb 2020   Aug 2020

🕐 Median tenure · 2.2 years

Rapid7 talent sources

Rapid7 hired 12 people from FireEye, Inc.. See all

Information Technology hires at   Information Technology hires at Rapid7
Rapid7 came from these companies   came from these schools and more
and more

In this example position for a Technical Account Manager at Rapid7, LinkedIn Premium shows you the following information.

- Competitive intelligence, how you stack up against the competition?
- Do your skills match what is needed for the position?
- How many other applicants there are for the position?
- What are the top skills for that position?
- What skills do you have that are relevant for the position?
- What is your level of the other applicants that have already applied?
- What are the other applicants' levels of education and position?
- What are the locations candidates are applying for the position?
- Inside Rapid 7's employees, is the company growing or downsizing?
- What is the median tenure of employees?
- Who does Rapid 7 hire from?
- Link to other contacts you might know.

All these pieces of intelligence can be applied to your search for a position.

You will not always find exactly what you are looking for, but the intelligence can be useful in crafting cover letters and resumes for positions you are qualified for.

Application insights help you to better position your resume and cover letter if you choose to instead apply directly to the job post on the company's website, or by contacting the hiring manager directly.

Premium can also provide intelligence on who viewed your profile and charts that go along with it to help you understand what impact your campaigns are having in making contacts. Users can still stay anonymous when they view your profile, but you will get far more insight than you do with the regular LinkedIn. When you have landed a new job, you can switch off your Premium membership and then turn back on the Premium membership if you need it again later. You will not, however, receive the free 30 days when you switch it back on.

Check out the screenshot below from LinkedIn Premium "Who viewed your profile."

Building Your Network Up and Out

If you are just getting started in your career, have been in your position for an extended period or are switching careers, the most desirable thing you can have, people looking at your LinkedIn profile. There are several ways to do this.

I put a lot of work into my profile and it shows. I have almost 1000 contacts before writing this book. This is mostly due to every person I work with directly; I invite to connect. And when I go to meetings with customers, I always look them up on LinkedIn afterward, and if they have a fairly complete profile, and I think they will be someone who can help me or maybe I can help, I connect with them. My Instagram and Facebook accounts have about 500 followers each and a post, even one of me and my kids doing something amazing, gets me about 20 likes and maybe three comments. Put in the work outlined below, because you need eyeballs on your profile to aid you in your job search.

It seems shameless to some people. I disagree, more than once has a contact been released from a job, and I was able to help them find new employment, because of a contact I have had in that area, or industry. It is not magic but just knowing someone who knows someone. It is simple and honest, you never know when a person you connect with will be able to say, "I heard ABC company is hiring, and I know Jeff over there. Give me your resume and I will talk to him for you." Doing that for others in the inverse, also is a super gratifying feeling.

We want to keep that honesty in who we are connecting with, so with an eye on growing our network and increasing our reach. We also need to be conscious of our industry, its partners, and its competitors because, in Section 3, we will be connecting with them to seek assistance in our job search. Connecting with 100 people authentically in a week will serve you better than connecting with 10,000 people who know you only from your generic LinkedIn invite.

- When you post on your LinkedIn feed, it goes out to all your followers if you have it configured correctly. To verify your settings, these are the defaults, go to Notifications > (on the top left, you will see a small text box that says Notification under that you will see "Improve your notifications") click View Settings > Communications (from the top bar) > On LinkedIn > Conversations Ensure the 2 red boxes are on.

  - If you are just starting to build out your profile for the first time, turn OFF Responses to your job updates to give you time to get all your wording and verbiage correct. You do not want to waste your follower's time with a job update from "to" to "too" in a job description.

- If you are leaving your position, by choice or otherwise, post a heartfelt thanks to all you have worked with and even if you do not have a true plan on what you will do next.

- Pro Tip before you do this, toggle on in your profile, that you are looking for work.

- "It is a bittersweet moment today for me at [company name], as I sign off the company network for the last time. Over the past [# years], I have learned so much through [accomplishment #1, accomplishment #2, accomplishment #3] and had the pleasure of working with some of the smartest, hardest working people in the [industry]. Thanks to [person 1, person 2, person 3, person 4, etc.], for all your dedication and support.

- The Grow Your Network Page allows you to sync your contacts with people in your address book on your email provider. If it is Google, Yahoo, or Outlook. This allows you to see who is on LinkedIn and invite them. I used this a long time ago and had many people in my contacts who were not necessarily business contacts. Congrats, you are now friends with your Aunt Genny, who has been retired for ten years, or worse other friends and family who do not understand the difference between an email, text message, and a public or private post.

- Write a short article or video and post it anywhere and then post a link to the article in your feed on LinkedIn. Good topics to cover
- What you are doing while looking for your new position.
- A condensed set of knowledge that will allow the watcher to get value. If you are looking for ideas and inspiration on this, check out "The Brutal Truth about Sales & Selling" on LinkedIn. I suggest the funny relevant content, but the sweat soaked shirt and panting are not required.
- Use Infographics about your industry you have made, or that you can link to that tell a story.
- Remember, "Pictures are worth 1000 words." Posts with pictures and text get more likes and comments than text alone.
- Write a short post in your LinkedIn feed and tell people what you are doing, in a positive way they might get something from that allows them to like or comment on.
- Watch who comments and likes the post. New contacts are what you are looking for.
- After a user has commented, be sure you go back and "like" the comment. This continues the communication between you and the commenter.

- Connect with anyone who comments or likes that is not already in your 1st level connections. This will increase your visibility into other 2nd and 3rd level contacts. These people will know you from your post and you will need to do a little cajoling to get them to accept your request.

- After the dust settles a little, and the likes and comments slow down. Go to My Network and look for people in your 2nd level network that you can connect with. Typically, your second level contacts will be people you have worked with. Do not be shy, some will outright accept your contact. Others depending on size and status of your network, will be hesitant.

- Include a note, although if you know the contact personally, it may not be necessary.

- For contacts I may not be familiar with, I typically include something like this *"Hi [LinkedIn User], I was reaching out because I saw you and [1st level LinkedIn contact] were connected and wanted to build my network in [industry or company]."*

- For contacts that I am looking for someone to help me get into a company *"Hi [LinkedIn User], We are both [company name] alumni and I saw that [LinkedIn users current company] has a [role or position] and I was wondering if you had a few minutes to talk about it?"*

- These are not musts, but it will help you with your overall numbers.

- Other important notes about requesting connections on LinkedIn
- You can request 3000 people to follow you.
- You can contact support if you need over 3000 requests
- You can and should withdraw requests that have gone for 7-14 days without a response.
- It has been challenging for me to find a hard-fast rule on "is it 3000 a day, week or month."
- Just do not spam 1000 people in one day looking to grow your network. This will get you a network of people you do not know, who do not know or care about you, which is exactly the opposite of what we are trying to achieve.

This is a good list, but it is in no way complete. There are tricks to amassing a following on any platform. We do not want to use tricks. The goal is good organic reach to people who can help us, and we can help later in return. When I made a recent post, my Who viewed your profile hit a huge spike, 177 views. I am not Jack Welch, or Jeff Bezos, but 177 views show a solid base of supporters. In that 177 people, someone has a job for you!

Who viewed your profile

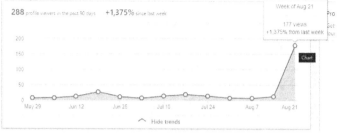

288 profile viewers in the past 90 days   **+1,375%** since last week

Week of Aug 21

177 views
+1,375% from last week

Chart

200
150
100
50
0
May 29   Jun 12   Jun 26   Jul 10   Jul 24   Aug 7   Aug 21

⌃ Hide trends

Research on Companies and People

There is a ton of research opportunities available on LinkedIn. This is the most important reason to be on the platform so that people can research you and you can find people to connect within your job search.

If you usually go into an interview with a potential employer, after a phone call from a recruiter or someone on the staff and do not know the industry or what the company does? Stop doing that RIGHT NOW!

As a hiring manager, if someone could not take the time to open a web browser and look at the website of the company, I am interviewing them for, they are wasting my time. With your situation, you cannot afford to waste anyone's time, including your own.

Do the research and be ready when asked about the position.

If doing good research helps you get a job. How come not everyone knows how to do it? You do, you just do not know how to apply it to your job search. We search Google every day for things we want or need, our restaurants, our choice of sneakers, the movie you want to watch on Netflix. Just think about that niche thing you are into, like car stereos. Would you just go out and throw your hard-earned money down on a car stereo because it has a good display, or what about the installer of the car stereo, are they known for doing quality work?

Most individuals never take the time to research their potential employer, but you should. The Mission statement we laid out in Section 1 says what? "Find a Fucking JOB!" We need a job because we need to keep the revenue stream flowing. What we also do not need is to find a position in a company that is not a good fit for us, with a bad culture or in a company not doing well financially, and turn around and be back here re-reading this book again.

425 employees

Search employees by title, keyword or school

‹ ... Next ›

Where they live	+ Add	Where they studied	+ Add
426	United States	26	Genesee Community College
278	Rochester, New York Area	23	Monroe Community College
86	Buffalo/Niagara, New York Area	18	SUNY Brockport
19	Elmira, New York Area	13	University at Buffalo
10	Syracuse, New York Area	13	State University of New York at Fredonia
5	India	12	Canisius College
5	Jamestown, New York Area	12	St. John Fisher College
3	Sacramento, California Area	12	State University of New York College at Buffalo
2	Redding, California Area	11	Rochester Institute of Technology
2	San Francisco Bay Area	10	University of Rochester - Simon Business School
1	Brazil	9	Finger Lakes Community College
1	Foz do Iguaçu Area, Brazil	7	SUNY Empire State College
1	Hyderabad Area, India	6	Nazareth College
1	Belagavi Area, India	6	St. Bonaventure University
1	Thanjavur Area, India	6	Keuka College

Show less ⌃

Researching Companies

Research will tell you if the company and position are a good fit for you. It can also make you look like a Rockstar on your resume, in your LinkedIn profile and, most importantly, in your interview.

Where can you get the info? Most of it can be gained in about 10 minutes on LinkedIn, Glassdoor, and Google. We will cover Glassdoor in the next chapter. For our purpose here, we will focus on three core things.

- Research on the company
- Research on the hiring manager
- Research on the position

LinkedIn is where you should start.

You and John are friends and John says his bank Star Bank is hiring. John will pass your resume along to the right person, so you have an internal champion there. John knows about the company work ethics and values and can relate them easily to you, so it sounds like a good fit and you send John your resume.

Sounds easy, right?

A week has gone by and Jane from Star Bank calls and says, "John gave me your resume and he is a great asset on his team, so I am sure you will be a great candidate if he is willing to recommend you. Tell me what you know about Star Bank?"

If you have never worked in the banking industry, have not looked at the bank's website, and did no research on the company, expect this to be your last call with Jane.

Here is how you start your research.

- Company website
- The rates for loans and accounts or other distinct features about the company.
- Their career page to see the job descriptions and if the job you are applying for is displayed
- The company motto, core beliefs and goals.
- See if they have any volunteer organizations they work with. I talk about volunteer organizations a lot but this is an easy way for you to find a commonality outside of the question about hiring someone because they are qualified.
- LinkedIn -- To the right, you will see the demographics from the company's public LinkedIn available with Premium.
- Make sure the company has a LinkedIn profile. Even small companies starting out will have one.
- Is the job posting on the website the same as the one you have seen on other job sites?
- Do you know anyone else working there?
- How many employees?
- Where do the employees live?
- Where did the employees go to college?
- What are their hiring trends?
- What is the median tenure of the employees?

This gives you a good starting conversation for your initial call with Jane or any hiring manager. Your understanding of the industry and the company will impress her.

Before you get to your interview with Jane, you should do your research on her as well.

Researching People

LinkedIn also allows you to find people to connect within your job search. It allows you to look at a company and see who in the company has a good chance of helping you or find the hiring manager for the specific job role you are looking for. The hiring manager is the one who makes the final decisions in your job search. Researching and connect will greatly increase your chances of success.

Why?

- It shows you are talented at making connections
- It shows you are interested in the company
- It shows you can do research with a goal in mind

When researching people for a new position, I start with the search bar of LinkedIn.

I search what I think the job title should be, in this case, "branch manager," and the company name I chose Star Bank for this search. You will need to refine your search to get the right set of matches.

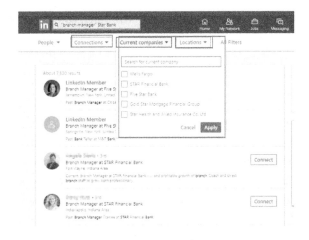

- When you first select the Search bar in LinkedIn, select People
- Input your search "branch manager" Star Bank hit enter and look at the initial results
- Narrow your search further and select Connections
- This is broken out in connections 1st, 2nd, 3rd
- Do not select anything here unless the company is over 1000 people
- Locations allows you to stay close to home by either inputting a location or selecting one from a drop-down
- Current Companies allows you to target specific companies that will be driven from your original company name in the search.

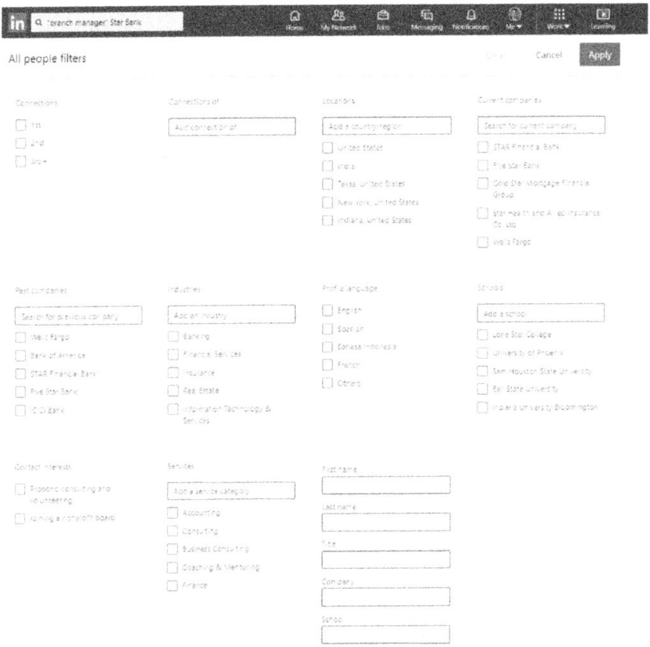
"branch manager" Star Bank
All people filters
Cancel
Apply

- For a complete list of filters, select All Filters
- Note the names that appear and if any are in your first, second, or third level network.
- Drill through each of the potential managers. You are looking for three things.
- An exact match to who you think the hiring manager will be who is on your first level network so you can connect directly with him or her.
- Someone in your second or third-level network on LinkedIn who can introduce you the hiring manager.
- Commonalities with people in the company you can bring into your first level network.

When you think you have found 1 person who could be the hiring manager, or a few people who can assist you in your job search, contact them. Be honest. Tell them who you are and why you are contacting them. I always try to keep it to a maximum of 3 lines. Like this

Hi [Contact Name]

We are both [Company Name] Alumni and I recently applied for a Technical Account Manager role at [New Company Name]. I was wondering if you had some time to talk about the role and how it compared to similar roles in other companies.

Starting the conversation is the hardest part. Be moderate with the number of people you contact. If you contact 50 people in a 100-person company, you will risk looking like a spammer, and not genuine.

I Can't find the company

This task is a little easier than it sounds.

Most job postings are listed on the internet to attract candidates in multiple forums and boards. Indeed, Google and LinkedIn should all have the jobs in one form or another from the company.

Let's say you've found a position that looks perfect, but it's advertised by a recruiter and the company isn't listed. You don't know whether you want to work there or whether or not there is someone in your network you can ask about the company?

With a little creativity in copying and pasting job descriptions into Google, you can quickly find the hiring company.

- Identify a position on LinkedIn. Indeed, Google Jobs or, Glassdoor
- Find 2 or 3 pieces of the job description that seem unique
- Search Google for the description text
- Chances are about 1/3 of the way down the page, you will find the hiring company.
- The first 1/3 will be all adds for other recruiting companies or job boards.
- Verify the company by going to the company's website and checking their career listings. There should be an exact match.

This method will work when the recruiting company is a small local firm or a giant global firm.

FINAL THOUGHTS ON YOUR LINKEDIN PROFILE

There are a lot of variables we do not address, like your industry-specific language as well as working time and time in the industry. My best advice there is to find another person in your industry with some similar experience and model your profile against theirs. Reread this, MODEL, **do not copy and paste**. You do not have the same experience and did not have the same lessons learned as anyone else.

LinkedIn is a professional business tool. Treat every contact or potential contact you are contacting like you would a coworker that you will see face to face at the office. LinkedIn users see your profile in their "Who's viewed your profile." If you see a guy or gal you fancy, do not contact them on LinkedIn, there are other platforms for that, just like you would not plop yourself down on a co-worker's desk and say, "What's cooking good lookin!" Keep it professional.

Everyone has their own beliefs and belief system. If you are a Democrat or a Republican. Love candidate X or hate candidate Y, IT DOES NOT MATTER. Unless you know them personally and they can help you in your job search, they are irrelevant to making sure you are employed. Do yourself a favor, help your job search and leave those views out of LinkedIn. We all have causes and politics we feel strongly about, but the cause you should feel most strongly about right now, is your job search and looking like the most viable candidate for every position you apply for.

I have not always been sensitive enough to other's perceptions or life experiences, and work on that to this day. What I do try to do now is listen more intently to people's points of view and allow them to express them without judgment.

In the upcoming Social Media section, I will discuss some of the DON'TS, remember LinkedIn differs from Snap Chat, Instagram, and Facebook. LinkedIn is where professionals come to network and find work or talent. No matter what talent you bring to the table, if you make your views so strongly evident that you could be more of a disruption than an asset in the workplace, it could be a silent disqualification.

In the On Lying piece in this section, I talk about how industry networks are small, and people know each other, do not sacrifice your integrity or reputation by doing something that could come back later as a negative.

Other Tools

These are more advanced tools that help you figure out if the company is a fit for you, how you are presenting yourself and how you are delivering that information to others.

Glassdoor

I was looking at working at a start-up in the Houston area. I knew someone was working there, I knew he would collect a sizeable amount of cash for referring me, and a lot of the details sounded good, a little too good. The initial call with their recruiter went well and I found several commonalities I could use to potentially secure a job, but there was just something about the conversation I could not put my finger on. I looked on Glassdoor and found that the number of negative views on the company, the products and the culture made it sound like a not fun place to work.

Glass Door is probably the most credible reference of company and internal workings, culture, and salaries.

Honest, candid feedback, with salaries, interview intel and benefits package information make it a great resource to understand what type of interview you will face, what a fair offer is and what you can expect when you get there.

- Companies – From the top menu bar of Glassdoor, the Companies menu allows you.
- Discover Companies. I found this to be highly location-based. If you are in a suburb of a major metropolitan area, choose the big city, not your local town. I could not really find a good option in here for remote work. This is probably due to the location bias some have when looking for a position.

- Compare Companies. You choose two companies and see how they compare on a list of topics important to employees of those companies. The categories range from Overall Rating, Career Opportunities, Benefits, CEO Approval and Work Life Balance. Another section talks about Salaries and a section for Employee comments. Check out the screenshots for a quick overview of what the companies break out looks like.

- Salaries are another area where Glassdoor excels. There are Salaries listed by job title and company. Salary Calculator allows you to fill out a short 4-5 question quiz then displays your approximate worth in an approximate area. Using this tool can help you determine if you are in the right range for salary when you enter the negotiation process of the job search.

Compare Uber vs Lyft BETA

See how working at Uber vs. Lyft compares on a variety of workplace factors. By comparing employers on employee ratings, salaries, reviews, pros/cons, job openings and more, you'll feel one step ahead of the rest. All salaries and reviews are posted by employees working at Uber vs. Lyft. Learn more about each company and apply to jobs near you.

Employee Ratings

- Uber scored higher in 9 areas: Overall Rating, Career Opportunities, Compensation & Benefits, Work-life balance, Senior Management, Culture & Values, CEO Approval, % Recommend to a Friend and Positive Business Outlook.

	Uber	Lyft
Overall Rating (full-time and part-time employees only)	**4.1** ★ ★ ★ ★ (based on 5045 reviews). Uber employees rated their Overall Rating 0.4 higher than Lyft employees rated theirs.	**3.7** ★ ★ ★ ★ (based on 527 reviews)
Career Opportunities	3.8 ★ ★ ★ ★ Uber employees rated their Career Opportunities 0.4 higher than Lyft employees rated theirs.	3.4 ★ ★ ★ ★
Compensation & Benefits	4.0 ★ ★ ★ ★	3.8 ★ ★ ★ ★
Work-life balance	3.9 ★ ★ ★ ★	3.8 ★ ★ ★ ★
Senior Management	3.5 ★ ★ ★ ★ Uber employees rated their Senior Management 0.4 higher than Lyft employees rated theirs.	3.1 ★ ★ ★
Culture & Values	4.0 ★ ★ ★ ★	3.8 ★ ★ ★ ★
CEO Approval	85% Dara Khosrowshahi Uber employees rated their CEO Approval 10% higher than Lyft employees rated theirs.	75% Logan Green
% Recommend to a friend	81% Uber employees rated their % Recommend to a friend 17% higher than Lyft employees rated theirs.	64%
Positive Business Outlook	57% Uber employees rated their Positive Business Outlook 13% higher than Lyft employees rated theirs.	44%

ERIN D. HUGHES

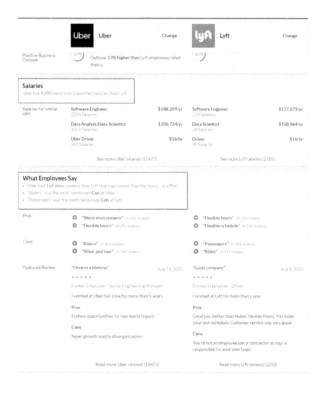

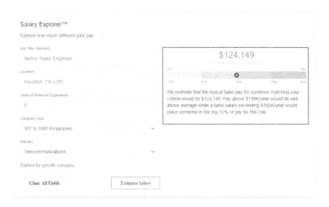

- Interview Questions Interviewing is hard and each company, just like each human, has a different approach to interviews and interviewing potential new hires. The Interviews section has good and bad intel on what an interviewing experience looks like when you go through it with a company as well as potential interview questions. As part of your interview preparation, you should be preparing yourself technically for standard industry interview questions, as well as the opinion and experience-based questions. Do not focus on the Gotcha type of questions "you have three tacos, and someone asks you for 2... How many do you have left?" Seriously those types of questions just test your metal under pressure. Check out the screenshot from some of the questions that get asked in interviews, and as part of your company research look through this section and

just mentally note what type of questions seem
more common.

cisco systems Interview Questions in San Francisco

Sort: **Relevance** Popular Date

---

cisco | Software Engineer Intern at Cisco Systems was asked...   Sep 10, 2013

There are ten buckets of lead weights, with nine of them having equal
weights of 10 grams each, while one of them has weights of 11 grams
each. You want to find out which bucket has weights of 11 grams each,
by using a scale, but you can only turn on the scale once.

3 Answers ∧   Gotcha Question

Actually pretty easy outside of an interview. Order the buckets. Then take zero
weights from the first bucket, one from the second, etc, and and add that to a
pile. Then weight this entire pile once.

@ Interview Candidate : how does that then solve the problem

I think the problem goes like --> All buckets have 10 weights of 10 gms each
and one has 10 weights of 11 grams each... If you number them 1 through 10 and
take equal no. of weights out as the bucket number. The ideal sum should be :
1*10+2*10+3*10+....+10*10 = 550. But since one of them is 11 grams. So, lets
say the 3rd bucket had 11 gm weights=> This means the total weight should
be 553 ... Hope this helps

---

cisco | Senior Software Engineer at Cisco Systems was asked...   Jul 21, 2012

Explaining Process Table

2 Answers ∧

---

where ?

San Bruno, CA   Bad Intel

---

cisco | Systems Administrator at Cisco Systems was asked...   Jun 21, 2010

What is the command that lists what files were currently in use?

2 Answers ∧

For Linux I would use lsof. List open files   Good Intel

---

lsof : is the linux command to list files currently in use

Glassdoor also posts new positions that are available, and the layout is good, but the volume is often not as high as Indeed or LinkedIn. Its real advantage is understanding company culture, parts of the interview process and typical salaries for a specific job role.

Remember, most people believe they know better than the CEO, the board, and their own manager. Be prepared for negative feedback on the company no matter how great the job sounds to you. Humans like to complain and the fact that the comments are anonymous just amplifies the safety factor people have to say whatever they want.

Take what you read on Glassdoor with a grain of salt but look out for multiple warning signs of toxic culture and bad management.

Resume

In the LinkedIn chapter, I said, "This is your resume in long-form."

A resume gets you your first phone call. A resume you craft for jobs and send out in emails is the concise version of the long-form representation of your LinkedIn Profile. A finely ground edge of a razor-sharp knife. It contains information on what makes you a great employee and why someone should hire you or at least talk to you about the position they are looking to fill.

Having a generic one size fits all resume, is a good place to start, then editing that to make it clear and concise for the position you are applying for is the goal. Tailor to target the advertised position, make it specific. Here are some pointers.

Refine your resume with these things in mind.

- 2 pages if you have 10 to 20 years of experience
- 1 page if you have less than ten years of experience
- Your name displayed (The biggest most prominent text on the resume)
- Contact Information Phone number, Address, Email address
- Positions held should be noted with
- Company Name
- Position Title
- Dates To – From I prefer a date format like 9 - 2014 to 12 -2018
- Brief description of duties
- Structure your resume duties section to define the problem, how you solved it and the outcome. See the LinkedIn section on Background/Experience to review how to clean up your job descriptions.
- If you have a 7-page LinkedIn profile
- List the top 4-5 most pertinent items at your previous employer.
- List the top 4-3 most pertinent items at your 2nd previous employer.

- List the top 3-2 most pertinent items at your 3rd previous employer.
- List the top 1-2 most pertinent items from the rest of your previous employers.
- If you have a certification pertinent to the position, list those towards the top, other certs can be listed towards the bottom.
- Make a resume you can send out at the drop of a hat to anyone and it conveys who you are and what you are capable of.
- Make a resume you can customize to send out to specific types of jobs you are qualified for.
- I have 20 years of experience – my resume is never longer than two pages. Never

For a copy of my resume here <u>Erin D. Hughes Resume</u>

For a copy of a formatted resume you can fill in <u>resume template</u>

Cover Letter

The unsung hero of the job search, your cover letter, or introductory email is your best shot to make a lasting impression on a potential hiring manager.

We can all write an email and contact someone about something we need or want. This is purely a transaction. You want something. You find someone to give it to you, you ask, they say yes or no. Anyone can do that but is that the extra mile to make someone go "DAMN I REALLY

NEED TO CHECK THIS GUY'S RESUME OUT!" Probably not.

We want to inspire someone to contact and connect with us not just because we need a job but more importantly because we can solve a problem they have, space in their organization they need to fill for the hiring manager and the company to succeed. Use positive wording and phrases that help us breakthrough, backed up with research that shows YOU are the person who can fill that slot, and solve that problem holding the hiring manager back from success.

Do you have abilities or skills that do not fit neatly into the narrative of a resume?

Good, your cover letter is an excellent place to highlight them!

Items like this are perfect call outs for your cover letter. It may be some volunteer work or something that did not directly fall into your job requirements or title that showcases your additional drive or abilities.

Here are a couple you could use to humanize yourself and stand out in the crowd.

Volunteer/Non-Profit Work shows you are a good human:

- I ran a PHENOMENALLY successful Toys 4 Tots Champaign 3 years in a row. With about 300 employees in the local office, we filled 3-4 boxes of toys and raised between $1000 - $4000 in cash donations each year.

- I am Director of Operations and Training for yearly STEM Camps through the Marine Corps JROTC where we train 150 – 200 Junior Reserve Officer Training Corps Cadets for 1 week on subjects that cover Linux, Windows, and Network administration, Python, Aeronautics, Robotics and Cyber Security.

Company based items are things most people might not know about the companies you have worked for and what they are known for. Use the accolades the companies you have worked for as an indicator of your drive and draw parallels to the company's excellence and yours.

- 7 years of experience working in Japan, at all Japanese companies like GMO, the largest ISP and Domain Name Registrar "Oname.com" in East Asia.
- Alert Logic, the leader in Cloud Security
- FireEye, Foresters leader in Threat Intel and Incident Response.

When making contact with hiring managers, our cover letter is our first impression, if yours says, "I saw you have an opening for a Senior Consultant, and I have been a Senior Consultant before." Stop.

In the LinkedIn section, we covered researching our connections with hiring managers.

Our cover letter should be a one size fits all, but when crafting your first draft, leave space for customization.

For a copy of my cover letter, click here <u>erindhughes-coverletter.pdf</u>

For a copy, an editable template copy of a cover letter, click here. <u>coverletter-template.docx</u>

Resume.com

If you have not had a resume or have been working at the same company a long time and have not had a need for a resume, you need a place to start. The Resumes & Cover Letters section offers my take on resumes. I have used these examples and templates to land some sweet jobs. However, if you are looking for another source, I suggest Resumes.com.

On the homepage, a guided tour helps you fill out your resume, but to skip that, scroll to the bottom and click the samples link that allows you to get access to all the samples.

The resume section offers 15 categories from Accounting & Finance to Emergency Services with multiple titles per category, allowing you to take multiple parts of different disciplines and combine them into something custom for you.

The cover letter section is even more complete with samples galore and a guided tour of a cover letter.

If you are starting from scratch, or not in an IT field which most of the examples in this book are geared towards, check out resume.com.

You can search by job title or industry and there is a wealth of additional information on formats and different approaches to your resume. Do not take my word for it; check out resume.com.

Job Scan co

ATS is a term I was not familiar with until recently. Applicant Tracking System is a tool used by employers to match key words and description details to your resume. Do not have the right set of buzzwords in your email, then look forward to getting a heartfelt no thanks email from the robot working in the back room of the employer you just spent an hour customizing your resume and cover letter to apply too.

JobScan is a tool that allows you to compare your resume to a job description and see how your resume would rate if they passed it through an ATS that filters on keywords and other algorithms.

In the next section, we will talk about competing on position and why it is a bad idea, however, if you do need to compete on position and want to make sure your resume gets through Jobscan.co is a great place to verify and refine your resume, so it is prepared to do battle with the ATS's of the world.

On the home page, scroll down to the option to either TRY SAMPLE RESUME AND JOB or Upload your resume to get started!

The Match Rate tells you how your resume faired compared to the job description you entered and gives you a list of items, ATS Findings, Recruiter Findings, Skills Matches and others that tell you what your score will be. The scan can also look at Cover Letters, as a premium feature.

Hard and soft skills can be scan for as well and ranked against the resume and job description.

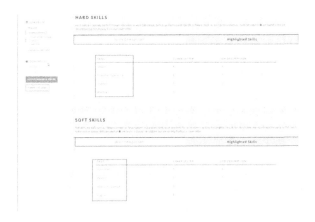

For Cover Letters, there is findings as well.

Word Count, Contact Information and Company Information are all covered, and Measurable Results and Words to Avoid are scanned.

The plans range from about 90 dollars for 3 months and 45 or so per month. There are also options out there for recruiters and career coaches starting at around 200 dollars a month.

I think it would be a worthwhile investment to make after all of your other contacts and leads dry up, or if you are looking at a company out of your geographic location where you do not have a contact who can help you get your cover letter and resume in front of the right person.

This tool can help when competing on position, but that is really the last place we want to compete.

Hunter.IO

Hunter IO is a clearinghouse for contact information on managers and executives. Primarily a sales tool to find contact information for industry leaders, it allows you to search by company name and individual name to see if you can find a match for an email address or individual. This combined with the next tool, makes contacting new contacts a lot easier.

The free plan allows you 50 domain searches a month for free and will give you the top names in that organization. The premium plan gives you a full list of names and emails as well as titles if they are publicly available.

Log in to Hunter IO and go to search. Enter a domain name and select all. This will give you a list of emails to populate your contact lists with. You can export this list as a CSV, so you do not need to search it again and again, if you have the premium account.

Here is an example search I did for Uber.

From the Uber.com domain, you can see the following information.

- Domain Search
- Total number of results
- Most common pattern for email address in the organization.
- A personal search box to refine your search to a specific person.
- Roles within the organization that have emails Selecting one of these fields brings up only the people in that role.
- The results
- Name
- Email
- The + icon allows you to add them to the Hunter IO system as a lead.
- The EMAIL icon allows you to integrate with Gmail and send directly from within the app from your search.
- The individual's title if available.

These results are very handy and can when combined with a little bit of research work on LinkedIn.

More about research will be available in the next section.

Yesware

My phone rang, from a phone number I did not recognize. I picked it up on the second ring and said, "Hello, David." David worked at a large Linux automation company and was calling to tell me he could not hire me because his company was just acquired by an even bigger Linux company. I knew this because I had been following the company on Twitter and LinkedIn and saw the news the day before. I knew it was David because my Yesware tracker for my follow up email I had sent David after our second phone interview, had just pinged on Chrome. David seemed surprised that I always knew when he would call and was intrigued enough to ask how I knew he would call.

"Yesware," I told him.

Yesware is an email tracking tool that allows you to see when your email has been opened and gives you a general location. It can also put the same type of tracking in PowerPoint presentations, word documents and even pdf's …. Like your resume. It is an invaluable tool to help you understand when you are getting serious traction within a company.

The pro package is about 15$ a month and totally worth it when you send an email see it was read, then see it was read some other location then see it was read on a cellphone. This does not happen on every email, but it does happen on the ones where you will potentially get a call, and it is an extremely exciting feeling. Check out this screenshot and you will see the email was opened in a couple of places by a couple of different people.

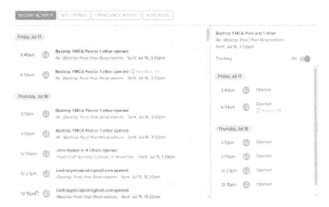

Besides the ability to let you know when your email is read, the Yesware website has a host of other features. Reports like the one below that show how often and when your emails are read or opened. Template folders that allow you to templatize your email correspondence and fill in the blanks where needed.

Finally, there are so many resources available on Yesware.com that allow you to use and understand the platform.

Even after I have used it for so much when I look at the training offered, I always feel like there is more to learn. Email templates, Reminders, and send later are 3 of my favorite features.

Another important thing to note is that each email you send out is a campaign. You are setting off on a journey with some new information to find a potential employer.

You can track these campaigns and see when the emails are opened, where and on what type of device.

With most companies having remote offices or workers looking at the campaign and seeing an email opened by an end-user in the location you sent it, say in Houston, then seeing it opened in 3 or 4 other locations on different devices does two things;

- It tells you the person is interested in what you had to say
- It tells you that person also forwarded the email to others for them to review.

This is the traction you are looking for. You have been able to interest people in you, and they are talking back and forth using your email to converse and make notes. The traction aspect is hugely important. It will let you know what works and what does not.

Pay attention to these numbers. If you send out a sloppily worded email or resume, expect it to get opened by the original recipient only. If you send a killer email that outlines your value proposition you will see the numbers rise.

Toastmasters

When asked about their biggest fears in life, what do you think most people say? Bears? Bees? Spiders? Getting shot? Having a car accident?

Public speaking.

One call where someone asked if I could meet that day to discuss a job, I walked in feeling confident and at ease, till I saw a former colleague from another company. He knew me before toastmasters and was the kind of person who would blurt in his objections in such a jarring and disruptive way it made speaking with him, a thing to avoid.

Although he was a bit toned down, his habit of disrupting speech patterns and interjecting was still prevalent, but I handled it all in stride.

Why? Toastmasters.

When something scares you, it can have a profound effect on the way you act and react to a situation, like being interviewed.

Being part of a Toastmasters club is one of the best things you can do for your interviewing and public speaking. The clubs offer a mature program that is easy to follow and with specific toll gates to help you improve your public speaking while creating confidence in your message.

Clubs typically meet once a week or once every two weeks, typically around lunchtime or after work. There is a set number of roles that everyone can or will be assigned before the meeting and a set number of speakers who get a specific number of MINUTES to speak on their topic and then it is discussed in a very regimented format.

Does this sound like something that would intimidate you? It should, just like a disruptive ex-coworker or an interviewer who likes to interject in the conversation unannounced.

To join Toastmasters, go to toastmasters.org and use the search function to find a club near you. There are open clubs and closed clubs.

Open clubs allow anyone to join and closed clubs are typically company internal clubs that are started out of an initiative to have better speakers within the company. Check out Toastmasters and level up your speaking ability.

I CAN NOT SAY THIS ENOUGH, DO IT NOW!

`We do not rise to the level of our expectations; we fall to the level of our training.

Archilochus

You and the Public's Perception of You

Talking about the things you post online and write down and deliver to the people in your network and you will allow you to take steps to be more proficient at helping others understand what type of employee you will be and what types of work you are capable of producing.

Social Media

Social Media today, is a great means of connecting you to the world. Having lived and worked in different locations with people of various views and cultures, the socials are a great way of staying in touch with friends and far away family members as well as seeing new, funny, and cool things.

Ask yourself, is your social media presence helping or hurting you in your job search?

Today everyone has an Instagram, Facebook, or Snapchat account. That was not always the case, 20 years ago. When you walked into an office, what the interviewer knew about you was written on your resume, and what you said during the interview, was how they judged you.

- Do you have highly active views and opinions that are vehemently expressed in social media?

- Do you wear your heart on your sleeve and advocate for people, are you staunchly opposed to specific political views?
- Heck, do you get blackout drunk and post pictures with you and your friends playing stupid games, and winning painful prizes?

You, as a person needing a job, need to look at your online footprint and determine, "Is there anything in this bucket of data that can hurt me?" The answer probably is yes.

2020 is a bit of a different world. A quick check of your LinkedIn that lists your name, a simple google search reveals your Facebook profile. The data others can gather just expands from there.

LinkedIn, Twitter, Facebook, Snap-Chat, Instagram … and whatever platform comes next is where people will be looking at you as an individual and how they will judge you.

China is working on a "Social Credit" system. Even if the rest of the world does not follow suit, employment companies will soon find a way to make your private social media activity part of the interview process.

If you face a negative life-changing event like losing your job or even something as small as a disagreement with your loved one or family, THE VERY LAST THOUGHT THAT SHOULD ENTER YOUR MIND IS COMPLAIN ABOUT IT ON SOCIAL MEDIA.

MINDSET Reminder, "Stop the bleeding …. get off life support"!

Even before you fill out your resume:

- Check your social media accounts
- Kick out any potential haters
- Remove any questionable content
- Lock down the access to only friends

This tail of WOW is about another applicant, and his social media presence was not his downfall but information that was openly available on the internet. Nathan was a bit odd and loved pro wrestling and online gaming, especially the game World of Warcraft. He was incredibly talented with MySQL databases, maintenance, and monitoring.

Nate showed up and to his credit, looked clean and presentable despite his patchy beard and long hair. He impressed the interviewers with his knowledge of SQL and Linux and general systems maintenance. Everyone shook hands and we all left feeling confident Nate would get the job.

We did not have a background check at the time that revealed anything more than a criminal record check. Anything you did on social media was up to our team to find and we performed our own search with basic data like your name, your phone number and email. The results from Google were benign and yielded nothing too captivating.

Then someone on the team searched WhoIs records.

WhoIs contains information about who owns a domain name. This was before the days when you could pay the Domain Registrar extra to hide your domain contact information.

WhoIs info for the domain looked like any other, name, address, phone number... are you kidding me? N#g##rsonline.com was registered to Nate. The domain listed his email and the cellphone number on his resume. No mistaking this was his work. I called him and let him know we would not be hiring him.

Do not be Nate.

On Lying

A close friend and I were recently discussing a position he had available.

We had talked about some candidates he had and was looking for pros and cons of each. He was using me as a sounding board to go through his ideas before he selected people for interviews. Turns out, I knew one candidate from a volunteer organization outside of work.

I liked the candidate personally, a good fellow to have a drink with; but on several occasions, he had volunteered for a role within the organization and had dropped the ball, often providing no forewarning he would not meet a commitment, and little to no remorse about having missed this event. I related that story to my friend and said he was good guy, but beware.

There were other external pressures to interview this individual, turned out he was a friend of my friend's Key Client. Before the interview taking place, though, this candidate had inflated a role on his resume just a tad bit by saying that that he had participated in a key role on a notoriously difficult project, when he held a much smaller role on a separate but related sister project.

During the interview, the candidate was asked about the specific events, times, dates, and locations the project occurred. The candidate again said that he had done these tasks, although at this point, my friend reported he sounded wishy-washy on his answers.

What the candidate did not know, was that one interviewer had been an assistant project manager on that project and had no recollection of him. Fortunately for the candidate, the interviewer was in a charitable mood. He called the candidate out on the lie, just to be certain. The interviewer was suspecting that perhaps his own memory may have been faulty, and the candidate may have had a very minor role. After checking the project records, down to the actual timesheets of who was employed where, the interviewer confirmed what he suspected: the candidate was lying.

Industry-specific circles are small, especially as you get closer to the top of those circles. Everyone knows everyone and if they do not know you, they can always call someone who does.

This book focuses on using your contacts to make inroads at a company for a position.

When people have a reason to suspect your integrity is at question, it takes away from them wanting to work with you. There are a lot of reasons you might feel the need to embellish something. The simple fact is it may help in the short term, but the long-term effects like damage to your reputation will not be worth it.

This candidate was not selected for the position, not based on any information I supplied but the hiring manager's question of his integrity.

SECTION 3

EXECUTION IS EVERYTHING

Without data, there can be no metrics.

Without metrics, there can be no measurement.

Without measurement, there can be no improvement.

Taborism

The MASTER List

In previous chapters, we have talked about improving parts of our online profile, our printed resumes, and our social media profiles, especially LinkedIn.

We have had friends and family contact us to aid in our job search.

We know of companies in our industry we can look to for new employment opportunities.

Time to put it all together.

The Master List is how you will track your job finding progress. This list is where the rubber meets the road and provides the hard data to show whether your job search is progressing.

The Master List is an Excel spreadsheet with 3 main tabs. A tab for the Contacts, Companies and Positions that allows you to track your efforts in one place.

Everyone's job search, contacts and interview process will be a bit different, just like every person you meet or company you work. Despite these normal variations, you can expect you will hit most of the major points in the job search workflows outlined below, but perhaps not every single one for your unique case.

CONTACTS, COMPANY, AND POSITIONS

Contacts

Our contacts are the most desirable area to hunt for new positions. Terms like "Everyone likes doing business with their friends." And "What are friends for?" help to cement the feeling that your friends will help you out.

Most companies have a generous policy regarding employment referrals, offering cash incentives or other forms of compensation to employees who bring in top talent. This will help incentivize your contact to reach out to others in his or her organization on your behalf and champion your advancement in the hiring process.

Using the Master List insert your contacts. Name, phone, email, company. Next, look at your contacts and understand them and how likely they will be able to help you. When we are done filling in the details in these columns, we can see who is best positioned to help us.

• Relation: Were you passing acquaintances, or did you work closely together? This has a 1 – 10 ranking with 1 being someone who you might know you if they saw you in person to 10 being a close confidant. We spend 8 or more hours a day with our co-workers, getting to know them better can help strengthen our relationships at work and help us outside of work, or as we seek our next position.

- Level: This 1 – 10 will help you understand and assess what level of influence your contact has, 1 is on a lower level of influence than you. A 10 can introduce you to the CEO and can block off time for the two of you to talk. This differs from a 4 who knows the name of the Executive Vice President of HR but could not introduce you to them.

- Value: What do you think they think of you as an employee, co-worker, or friend. Those friends that will stick their own neck out for you, and go the extra mile to help you, 10's. Contacts who will casually forward your resume to a hiring manager with an open position but won't follow back up with that hiring manager, that person is a solid 5. Others who know you well enough to say you are a good guy or gal but will not stick their neck out any more than that rate lower than a 5.

These are all just guesstimates, be brutally honest while filling out each contact's score, especially in the Value category.

Next, we will use their score to determine who we should talk with first. The total number will appear after you have scored the contact, in the Rank column. When we have filled in the score for all our contacts, I would start with your top 25, we will sort by the Rank column from highest to lowest score, and that is where we will start reaching out.

The spreadsheet will score the contacts with a Rank as soon as you fill in the contacts scores. Scores in the Rank column will be rearranged automatically when you refresh the spreadsheet or switch back to the Contacts sheet from another tab.

On the Contacts sheet, ALL the data is important!

Fill it in. Although it is not noted in the screenshot in the note's column, I try to put a link to the contact's LinkedIn profile. This provides an easy means of refreshing your memory on the contact before you reach out. With the sheet refreshed, you will see your most valuable contacts.

The Company column is extremely important!

Ensure you put in the exact company name. This will be used in the other sheets to populate contact information. If you use abbreviations or shorthand like GE for General Electric or some other nickname, this will show up in the Company and Positions sheet when you use the dropdown. More on this later.

Expect a few bumps and bruises from reaching out to contacts, and yes, you will feel uncomfortable reaching out to contacts you may not have spoken to in a few years, we all do, but do it!

> *You miss 100 % of the shots you don't take.*
>
> *—Wayne Gretzky*

Once a contact has pleasantly surprised you by offering help, it's important that you realize and respect that their recommendation of you works both ways. That is, their reputation with their employer is on the line if you flake out. Early in my career, I had relied upon a contact who had proactively recommended me for a couple of different positions in his organization and even a couple he knew of through his network outside of his organization.

In one case, I was not only late for the interview, I failed to prepare properly and just plain SUCKED!

I did not practice interviewing and failed to gather even the most basic background information on the company. The next time I reached out to this contact for help, it was complete radio silence.

Basically, I failed my contact in multiple ways, and he did not want to be embarrassed again. I also botched reaching out after the poor interview. I did not try to correct mistakes in my interview and did not perform the follow-up actions of thanking people for their most valuable commodity, TIME.

Contacts, next to time, are your most valuable resource, do not squander either.

Company

The second-best vector for your job search is other companies in your same field. If you are in sales, you already understand who the competition is and what makes their offering different from your previous employer.

Non-sales professionals may not readily understand the competitive differentiators between two companies but understanding the work processes and underpinning technology that make your industry run has its own value. Your experience will be key in helping your search.

On the Master List under Companies, you will see these fields:

Date – The date added to the Master List

Relation – How does this company relate to your previous company? Are they a customer, supporting company, partner, or direct competitor? Add in how they relate to your past company. Then when you need to, you can sort through the list of companies by this field and better understand where you have more contacts.

Company Name – This dropdown will auto-populate from the Contacts sheet. If you do not have a contact at the company, then type in the company name.

Contacts – First, Last, Email and Phone # Do you know anyone who works at the company you are looking for a position with? The contacts field will auto-populate if there is a contact working in the same company. This will allow you to see who to reach out to in the company when you find a position to apply too.

Link to Career Page – This should be the general career page. This way if a new position is not emailed to you by LinkedIn or another source you can just click and check for new positions.

Apply – Y/N Have you applied in the past to the company?

# of Contacts – If you know more than one person working at the company this field will populate

automatically. You can circle back to the Contacts sheet and see the other contacts if you need too.

Notes – In here, you should put any relevant information about the Company you need to remember, what is their market differentiator, what is the motto, etc. If the company calls, you can pull up these notes as a reference.

The Company spreadsheet is mostly for a reference. It shows you where to search for contacts you do not currently have. LinkedIn can help you look for company employees who you may have work with previously. Those past employees can turn into contacts who you can reference later.

Take a moment, think about all the competitors in your field. List them in the companies' page. Look for supporting companies and partners. Your knowledge of the inner workings of your previous employers will give you an edge and these companies know it. Look for good references in your previous employer that have connections to people in the companies on the list you have created.

The company tab is to help us track the progress of our contact search. As you build your network, and your Contacts tab gets filled out more completely, you will see how they relate or can help you in your search inside of a company.

Notice the Company dropdown on the Master Lists Companies Sheet. It was highlighted earlier, but it can be used to help you understand what contacts work in

Companies you are looking at and to give you a frame of reference for who you should be reaching out to.

This is stated in this part of the chapter twice, once in the beginning and once at the end. It is the main point of building out the Companies sheet and is meant for reference as well as encouragement.

Position

The last place you want to compete is against other applicants, for a position. This literally means you saw a job posting and you thought, "I can do that," and you applied for it. These positions are posted for the world to see and everyone who thinks they are remotely qualified will respond.

Once upon a time, there was a unicorn job, an English-speaking Unix Engineer job in a large well-known company in Japan. Japanese language ability was not a criterion, Unix skill was. Every gaijin in Tokyo who could spell UNIX applied to this job. At one count, there were over 500 resumes.

The hiring manager was ordered to review all the resumes. He printed them out and made a huge stack. He shuffled the stack, making sure there was no preference for alphabetical names or any other numbering system.

He cut the resumes like a deck of cards into two piles.

When he was happy that both piles were the same size, he paused, looked at the piles, grabbed one pile, picked it up ……. and threw it in the trash.

He turned to the rest of the team watching in disbelief and remarked, "I never want to work with anyone that unlucky," while pointing at the pile of resumes in the trash. Everyone looked puzzled, then he said, "Find me someone in this pile. Someone in there has better luck" and walked off.

No one in either pile knew the hiring manager, a different department's manager, or any other contact (useful or otherwise) in the company. Everyone was competing on position.

Now this story is over 15 years old; no one prints out all the resumes and compares them to other job seekers even at exceedingly small firms. As we outlined in Section 2, there is automation to weed out people who they do not feel align to the job description.

Competing on position with no contacts in the organization you are applying to makes it exceedingly difficult to differentiate yourself from other applicants. When applying simply on position it is best to have all the research and knowledge built up ahead of time.

Not that it is impossible or unheard of, but the goal is to find another job quickly. The goal is to have our contacts sell us internally to the hiring manager so we can have a casual conversation about skills and outcomes we provide.

The goal is to differentiate us from everyone else in the pack, clearly.

If you find a position that you think you should apply for in a company that you have no contacts inside of, and all of your other resources have been exhausted, throw the dice and apply anyways but do it only after you have exhausted all your Contacts and Companies.

The Positions tab is the scorecard for all the positions you have applied for. Put all the information into the Position you have in the positions tab.

Date – when did you apply for the position

Position – This is the technical name for the position.

Company – Choose from the dropdown or enter a company name.

Contact—Contact information First, Last Name, Email, Phone # are all filled in automatically if the contacts information is in the Contacts form.

Link to Position – A link to the open Position

Apply – Did you apply for the position Yes/No

# of Contacts – This number will be auto-populated with the number of contacts who work at the same company.

Level of Confidence – On a scale of 1-10, how likely are you to be called to interview for the position. Remember in the 2nd Section on LinkedIn Premium and researching people?

Response – Was there a response from the company?

Follow Up Date – Date, typically 5 business days.

Notes – Any information that could be useful on the position or company.

The Positions sheet is not only for jobs you have applied for that you had no contacts in. It should include every position you applied for.

The same principles apply as in the Company sheet. Fill out every Position you apply for and the Master List will populate the Contact column with names of contacts you have Contacts in. If there is no contact, you can fill in the Company name.

Ensure you are tracking each position you applied for with a Level of Confidence, Response Y/N, and a Follow Up Date.

This will help you understand what you should file each position as, In Process, Rejected, No Response or Waiting.

In Process is exactly how it sounds; you have had communication and are waiting for next steps or an interview or offer.

Rejected is a polite no thank you from the recruiting ATS.

No Response is just that, you fired off your email or applied online and heard nothing so far. Do not give up on these, sometimes they take time. Keep looking for contacts inside the organization. If it has been 3 weeks or more, file it as rejected. If a company takes 3 weeks to put you in the hiring pipeline, it may not be a fit for you.

Waiting is a hard thing to do. This indicates you have a contact or received an email but have had no follow up. Waiting status typically means reaching out weekly to make sure they are still interested.

You will quickly see that positions without contacts will have little to no traction.

John made an extra sheet and tallied up the results for one month.

He recounts the tale of August in the section below that should cement the idea that finding a contact as an internal champion is the best way to go. He had applied to 36 positions during one month. Of those 36, he only received 3 positive responses and had 33 of his resumes either not respond to or rejected.

August Positions:		
Companies Applied to	36	
Blatant Reject	4	11.11%
More Info (i.e., Call from HR):	3	8.33%
No Reply at all	29	80.56%

Three answers out of almost 40.

That is a soul-crushingly small positive response rate. This does not mean I expect to talk you out of sending out resumes for random positions; but it is not an efficient use of time. Applying for each position takes time, let's say an average of an hour each to search and find a position you're interested and or qualified for. Those hours could be better used on networking and creating contacts you want to work with.

In Section 2 we detailed the method to have LinkedIn send you positions relevant to your job search. And Google Jobs also have similar features. Use those instead of trolling through every position available and save your time and sanity.

Position based searches can also lead to situations where you know the company and it has a good reputation, so you want to work there, even though you have no contacts in the company. That you will take a "Close Enough" approach to a position might occur to you.

Here's how this strategy typically plays out. I have been in consulting for about 14 of my 20 years in IT. I have all the necessary skills to be a Technical Account Manager.

Reading my resume, you would notice I am not nor have I ever been part of an account management team. During a past job search, I applied for a position as a Technical Account Manager at a large internet networking company, thinking it would be a foot in the door, instead, I was quickly rejected as being overqualified for the position.

Overqualification is a real thing, hiring managers understand it because they know that you will quickly get bored with tasks associated with a role you can perform easily, and will want to move up or on to another company.

If you are thinking sooner or later that a Company with multiple open, lower level or entry-level Positions available may eventually have a position you are interested in and ideally qualified for, you could apply for then, level up internally.

Do not apply.

Nothing shows you are an unstable career butterfly than when that Company's candidate screening system shows that you've already applied for several jobs well beneath your skill level like Fry Cook, Head Janitor and Junior Code Analyst, when you are more qualified for a Senior Programmer position.

You think you'll get a foot in the door and dazzle them with your brilliance. This isn't a Lifetime movie of the week; it is the real world.

Do not waste your time and a possibly better opportunity later with the same company unless you are prepared to dumb down your resume and take a serious pay decrease.

Remember our Mission Statement **"To find a new position that will allow me to provide for my family at or near our current lifestyle."**

If you are still thinking you need to spend more time on positions than reaching out through the contact list, let me add a follow up to the chart above.

What you can't see from the above data is what John found out in his initial phone screening from his most promising response to a Position was revealed to him in the initial interview that his resume had been spotted and highly recommended by, you guessed it, a contact who remembered him positively and who himself had only been with the company two months and had neglected to update his linked in profile. Focus on your contacts first!

Finally, before you send out a bunch of resumes and cover letters for positions, remember our lessons from section 2 on ATS.

Take the job descriptions you are applying for and then match them with a copy of the resume you plan to send in JobScan.io. This will at least give you a chance and just because you do not know the hiring manager today, does not mean you cannot find him or her later in the process. Press forward and do not give up easily on a lead unless you find a dead end.

Putting it all together

Going through all these steps, you must be thinking to yourself, "Erin, did you really do all those things from day One?" and the answer is "of course not!" The entire system around how I track contacts, jobs and companies evolved from the sheer chaos that erupted over the first couple of days.

I had a ton of contacts.

Those contacts had contacts.

Those contacts led to company and job searches.

I applied, emailed, and called so many people that without some concrete way of tracking them, I was essentially blind to what call I would be on next with what company or what contact. It made following up after I had seen my email opened difficult.

Somewhere around day three or four of my job search, in a one-hour time span, five different contacts at different companies opened emails, forwarded emails that were first opened by someone else that pinged in Yesware, or replied to messages on LinkedIn.

This is not a huge amount of information; but there was no structured system for prioritizing my next actions or a scoring system that ranked and prioritized my contacts. I was handling them all in a first in first out type of method and spent the next two hours of that day replying to another job posting that caught my eye.

What I should have been doing was striking while the iron was hot and following up with the LinkedIn contacts that had responded and then studied the companies that had shown interest in my resume and cover letter by opening the mail and forwarding it.

By the end of the first week, in full panic mode, I sat down and started cataloging:

- Who did I call/email?
- What companies was I looking at applying to?
- What positions had I applied to?
- What were the outcomes?

Having the data in front of me also provided an inverse benefit; it showed me where I was not getting responses and thus, where I should stop wasting time.

One contact, who I had worked with before and had referred to several people when he was seeking employment, reached out steadily for a week after my initial departure. While his daily calls were a needed bit of encouragement, the spreadsheet helped me recognize that the introductions he offered never materialized into interviews or further contact introductions. With the hard data in front of me, I recognized that our daily calls were turning into nothing more than a way for me to distract myself from more productive job searching. I stopped taking those calls when I figured this out.

All this work will be worth it, not only in terms of a more productive job search but in the name of your sanity as well! It is a system, and like all systems it requires discipline and work to update and maintain. I promise you though that sticking to the system will produce results.

Not convinced?

Let's have one more look at the "traditional" job search alternatives: Writing a resume for the first time since you needed the last one, probably a few years back, and then firing off that general "one-size-fits-all" resume to any Company that posts a job on the internet you are remotely qualified for. Or spending an hour or more squeezing your resume into a recruiter's 99-page data-entry form with 50 required fields and 20 EULAs, so someone can discount you in a couple of keystrokes because you do not have experience with an ancient piece of software. It is the same as having your resume in the "Unlucky Pile."

Then after the resume or recruiter's cover sheet has been received, what happens? The years of relevant experience you diligently shoe-horned into a two-page resume format are ignored or discounted because the hiring manager could not clearly articulate what systems were important and what were only "nice to have" to the recruiter or Applicant Tracking Software system that screened your resume.

The system is in place to do one thing. Drive efficiency and allow us to be more productive. Use the system to get hours back you would lose on filling out forms and customizing your resume.

Get that time back and work more efficiently.

WORKFLOW

Contact Based Search

With the contacts sheet filled out, we get into the workflow of how to handle reaching out. The flow chart below shows the steps involved in using a Contact Based Search. For a copy of this search workflow click here.

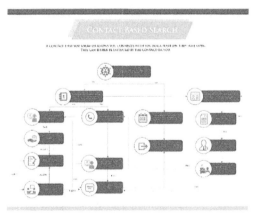

Contact Based Position Search Q & A

Look at the values you have assigned Contacts in the Master List. When the contacts are sorted by rank, you will see who stands out on the top of the list.

At first, to get warmed up, pick the lowest 5 contacts, especially ones you have not spoken to in a while. Use them as practice tests for your initial cold emails and calls. After you have your cold call/email down, focus on the top 5.

What should you prioritize calls, texts, emails, or LinkedIn messages?

Calls – Great for a friend or someone you have worked with closely and you know can be counted on to pick up the phone when you call if they are free and provide value. Consider the person's schedule when calling. Try not to be intrusive about the time you are calling.

Text Messages– Texts are a great medium to communicate with someone if they are an acquaintance who will reply to you on your schedule. It is also an easy unintrusive way to get in touch without demanding a conversation right now.

Emails – This is a more formal request. It provides a bit more formality and allows a bit more substance to be communicated and allows additional information to be added in the form of resumes as attachments. It is also an omnipresent form on almost every phone or computer, so it makes it easy to reply.

LinkedIn messages – I like LinkedIn messages for strangers when reaching out and making the initial communication that moves to another form, like email or phone calls.

Develop a script – Like every other lesson in the book for the above communication methods described above, have a script written down beforehand about what you want to communicate and what you want the outcomes to be.

Practice – Just like we will talk about in the next sections on interviewing, we can take some of the pressure off ourselves in the initial conversation by practicing with a friend or family member beforehand.

Then just do it – Schedule a time and make calls, sending the texts, emails, and LinkedIn messages.

With an email, phone call, or meeting request. As soon as you have been in touch with the contact, do not waste time and get right down to business.

- Does the contact have a position you could fill?
- Are any of the positions a good fit?
- What is the company culture like?
- Is the contact willing to represent you or introduce you to the hiring manager?
- Is there a bonus or compensation for referrals?
- Even if they are not willing to do that, will they put you into the HR workflow?
- Does the contact think you have the skills to work in the position they have available?

- If yes to all of those, then start down the preparation routes outlined below.
- Whatever stage you exit the workflow, take notes.
- Noting what you did right and wrong will give you intelligence on what is working and what is not.
- Finally, do not forget to send out the Thank You emails to your main contact and anyone else involved in your interview process.

This, next to interviewing, is the hardest section in the book. It does not take a degree in Astro Physics. It just takes guts and doing that can be a little challenging. Remember having someone you know who is on your side will make a huge difference in getting into the hiring pipeline, and this is the quickest route to getting in.

Company Based Search

For Company based searches, it is best to locate a company in your industry where you know you already have the skills required to perform the work associated with the positions they would likely advertise, then look through your contacts for people who can connect you inside that company.

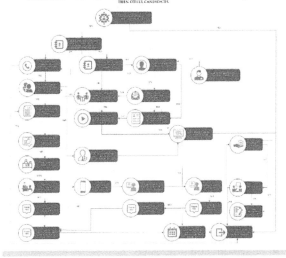

The Company Based Search Q & A

Companies in the company workflow can be referenced by the

- Listing customers, competitors and supporting players in your industry and then looking for contacts in the company.
- Do you have a contact in the company?
- What does the company do that you can relate to?
- Can you use LinkedIn or Hunter IO to find a contact?
- When you find the contact, are they open to talking or meeting?
- No, but still interested
- Yes
- Is there a position open in the company?
- Is the position a match for you?
- Will your contact put you into the HR pipeline and recommend you?
- No contact, use Scan.IO to make sure your resume matches the keywords in the job description?
- With or without a contact in the company, do you feel your skills are strong enough on paper to get you an interview?

Position Based Search

For position-based workflows, you have no contacts to start, but you can try to make them as you work through the process. Be patient when reaching out and try to make sure that you give new contacts enough time to respond; 5 business days should be enough. Less time is needed if you see a contact has seen your email in Yesware or has read your message on LinkedIn. Then if you get no response, you need to go it alone and apply directly to the position.

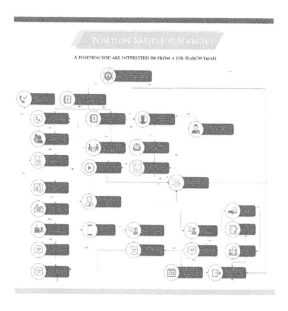

This is the most complex of the searches because you are starting from zero. You have no contacts or no inside company info. You saw a posting for a position you think you can do, now you need to figure out where to start. If you are lucky and you have been filling in your Contacts sheet, you will see there is a contact who works at the company and you can connect with to discuss the position. That is not really luck, that is you doing your homework and diligently outlining your contacts. If you have no contacts in the company, ask yourself if I use LinkedIn or Hunter.IO, can you find one?

The Position Based Search Q & A

- Does the Position look like a fit for you and your skills?
- Does the Position look like something you could be phenomenally successful at and provide value to the company?
- Does the company have a good reputation for hiring and management decisions? (Check Glassdoor and other news about the company.)
- Do you have a contact inside the company or think you can find one of your current contacts has a contact inside the company?
- Can you use Hunter IO or LinkedIn to find a new contact at that company?
- Have you taken a copy of your resume and modified it using jobscan.io to help it get through the ATS system?

WORKING BACKWARDS TO GO FORWARDS

One contact who tried the techniques in the book found that all the work in the front end of the book was a pain. He wanted to spend more time hunting for positions. He felt like finding more positions would lend him more opportunities for success.

I initially tried to keep him on course, but as a consultant, I finally let him do it the way he was comfortable.

In the end, he found a position; it took about 55 working days. Not bad, but when I asked him about his workflow, he was clear.

- He found a position he thought would fit.
- He then researched the company, and if he thought it was still a fit, he would move forward.
- He had a noticeably clear vision about the type of company he wanted to work at, Cyber Security, small startup with an everyone-does-everything kind of work environment, between 100 to 300 people.
- Finally, he would send out his resumes without a contact or internal champion of any kind.

His resume and LinkedIn profile were good, and he was professionally qualified.

When he did land his position, he was incredibly pleased and thanked me. He did not follow my plan for success, so his accomplishment was solely his own.

When I asked him how many positions he had applied for, I was floored…. 143.

If an application for one position takes roughly an hour, and he had no outside help from contacts in the industry. That was 143+ hours spent applying to "Just the right position/company."

As we wound up our last call together after he had accepted the position, he said, "But you know, Erin, I think next time I will take your advice, the place that I did get the job at, I didn't know this at the time, but they had hired 3 people from my previous company. One that I use to work with closely, and when he saw my resume come through HR, he flagged it as "Someone we should hire." He went on, "If I had known my friend was there and spent the time putting in the work, as you say, going through my contacts, I would have had that position in 2 weeks."

The advice and tales you have read in this book, are life experiences my friends and I have been through and at this point, they have all used the lessons in *45 Days to Hired* in one way, shape or form. They all now recognize that the initial effort that first day of cultivating all of your contacts, understanding the companies in your industry and then looking at the positions they have to offer will get you to the same place as hunting out positions and blindly applying, but it will get you there faster, with less effort and less stress.

Hiring in the real world

Let's take a moment to examine a highly misunderstood aspect of job searching, what happens to your resume after it's in "the system." We all hope that when a company posts a job, the hiring manager is busy diligently reading each resume that crosses their desk hoping to find the perfect fit. Let me assure you, this does not happen…. anywhere. The hiring manager still has a day job; this is one of the many reasons HR departments are created. If a position is open, we can hope that the position was created because the manager had enough foresight to predict a need based on the expanding volume of business at his or her company and budgeted for that need. The hiring manager has worked smartly to back-date this position's desired onboarding date to allow time for onboarding and training for the new hire to get up to speed.

If XYZ Corporation is like most companies, even some of those Fortune 500 and "Most admired" workplaces lists (Companies where you would assume they have their business in order), when a job hits LinkedIn or Indeed.com, the following has most likely happened:

1)   "Oh Crap, we just won a project we weren't really expecting, now we're shorthanded, what a great problem to have!"

2) "Oh Crap, Bob or Janice just left for a better paying/more time off/closer to home job offer when we thought they'd put up with our shit forever.

Remember, in either situation the Hiring Manager is being evaluated by their own boss on:

1. How quickly they fill those urgent needs.

2. The quality of candidate they find.

You can well guarantee that when a job does hit the job search website, said manager has already exhausted their own collection of contacts and is now in "get this done quickly mode."

After you have spent hours crafting "the ultimate resume." You have blindly sent it to 30 prospective employers this month. In my experience, an average 80% of those 30 employers rejected your resume upon receipt because it did not fit their ATS profile or their HR Recruiters reward system (Finding **any** fit quickly, not the **perfect** fit).

Now, which position do you want to be in?

Having invested precious hours into a dead-end search effort only to pull out what is left of your hair because 80% of the time, your resume isn't even read by a human being? Or investing a fraction of that time crafting an organized system to focus your efforts on the opportunities with the highest percentage chance of reviewing your resume.

Yes, it does take some actual work and thinking up front.

By now, I hope you recognize how important it is to have an internal champion for your job search. Someone who knows you and can articulate your value, while also having enough influence in the organization to sway people to your side.

Work the system….work your contacts…work competitors or other supporting players in your field and then if you strike out on all of those, search for positions, but only then.

Side note: It should come as no surprise that when I was a hiring manager, I was astounded at how infrequently my input was sought to craft detailed job descriptions for the position I was hiring for. When I did offer input, it was frequently ignored because the recruiter had their own metrics they were being graded upon, which did not include finding me the "perfect" candidate, and found it easier to pull a generic job description from the corporate catalog.

IN THE PIPELINE

You have gone through a handful of duds in the Contacts, Companies and Positions and have found an interested hiring manager or internal champion to help you go from being just another piece of paper or candidate to someone who is known and can potentially fill a need in the company you want to apply to.

There are 2 ways this can happen.

Internal Champion – This is the hiring manager or a contact who works at the company who wants to help you get on board so you can help them with a pressing need.

Successful Resume Submission – You have submitted your resume and it made it past the ATS system and have been contacted by an internal recruiter.

Congrats, you have passed the main hurdles to getting noticed. Just getting someone at your target company to know who you are. Now is the time to get into the next steps of fulfilling your quest for gainful employment. The next 20 plus pages outline strategies to keep you in the pipeline and help you complete the interview process.

Pre-Interview

You have gotten to the hiring manager or someplace in the recruiting pipeline. Most companies, especially in 2020, are more interested in phone interviews and Zoom or WebEx style meetings. Typically, there are 3 phases to these interviews.

Remember this is not a one size fits all prescription. Sometimes there will be 2 initial screenings, one with HR and one with the hiring manager. Other companies will do an all at once approach that will have a marathon of interviews on the same day. These are company and department-specific, so be prepared and be flexible.

Having the right level of knowledge and skill as well as honing your experience, to fit into a few easily relatable stories you can use to convey your knowledge and how you handle difficult problems that align with the company's core values. Doing them correctly is make or break for you, so read them closely and be prepared to make notes on what areas you think will help you.

INITIAL PHONE SCREENING – A recruiter will call you and ask about the position and your goals, also making you aware of the interview process and what is coming next. During this part of the process, you will also be asked about salary expectations.

Try to reframe the question to the recruiter with something like, "What do you feel someone with my experience and knowledge will be worth to you and your company?" The recruiter will typically come back with a salary range they are looking at for the open position. Reply with what you feel is fair. It is important you remember this, decide, and stick with it.

An important caveat here: We've all seen the "good" advice about playing salary hardball and never admitting to how much you want in a first phone call, or before a firm offer is placed in front of you. Let me say, that's a bunch of dangerous garbage, especially when you are in the position of "holy shit, I've just been let go."

As a hiring manager, I always conducted my first telephone screeners with a checklist of questions to ask each candidate, and one of the first of those was about salary range expectation so we could cut the shit up front and make sure we weren't wasting time for either of us due to a mismatch in expectations. Remember, your recruiter does this every day…. for a living, unless you're applying for a job as a professional negotiator, the Recruiter probably has much more experience in haggling than you do. Offer an acceptable range you can live with, and under no circumstances tell them a sob story like, "Well, I **need** at least $100,000 to make ends meet."

Making your ends meet is well below last place on the Recruiter's priority list. It makes you sound desperate and desperation is never attractive in a job candidate.

TECHNICAL SCREENING – An individual working in the role or works with the team will call you and ask you questions based on your work experience, and technical questions related to your field and your goals.

After you go through a few technical screenings, if you have a decent amount of awareness, and technical skills in your job, you will see there is a pattern to the questions you are asked. A quick Google search for "Network Engineer interview questions." There are plenty of examples out there.

Now search for "[whatever you're chosen profession is] interview questions." Pick a couple of the top links and study and review the questions. Understand how to answer them, what technical skills they demonstrate and slight variations of the question.

I know this sounds ridiculous, but we are trying to ensure we succeed. Do not let something you know but could have easily studied trip you up.

I used Solaris, a UNIX operating system when working in Tokyo for a couple of years. I am no Solaris pro but learned a lot from the experience.

When an opportunity came to interview someone who had put they had 10 years of Solaris experience on their resume, I thought it would be a cool chance to geek out a bit. There was little application for Solaris in the role, but generally, UNIX administrators can adapt to Linux administration easily.

In the phone screen, I asked, "How do you configure a network interface on Solaris?"

There was a stammering and a bit of "ummm aaaa" on the phone.

Frustrated, I asked, "Tell me about what you did with Solaris?" After 2 to 3 minutes of non-answers, I asked mostly out of curiosity, "Why did you put it on your resume?"

"Because people with Unix skill get hired." Yes, they do, he, however, did not have any and was not going to be hired.

The person who does your technical screening will probably read your resume the closest. Anything on there is fair game, and you should be able to talk about it.

When I did technical screenings, I had 10 questions of increasing difficulty, most people only made it to 6 or 7. I also asked 3 questions based on technologies they worked on in the past. If you got 1 wrong, maybe it was the way I asked it. If you got 2 wrong, I was suspect and might ask an additional one for clarity. If you got all 3 wrong, your resume went into the trash or bit bucket, as we say.

This information is here to make you aware that usually, the technical questions you will get in the screening are difficult for a reason. They are trying to find the truth in your resume.

Did you work on a specific technology or was it the responsibility of the team you worked on and you never really touched it.

You have been warned, prepare yourself to be better than what is printed on your resume.

IN PERSON INTERVIEW OR VIDEO SCREENING –

The meat of your interview process. Review the company's website, understand their business model and be ready with facts and data about their industry to help display your skills and preparation for the role.

Here are some steps to make sure you knock every part of it out of the park.

Be ready – Before

ROLE-PLAY BEFOREHAND– If a friend works at the company, have them give you a mock interview and ask questions based on what they think you will be asked. If you know no one at the company, ask any friend or acquaintance who can listen and suggest to you what to say.

BE POSITIVE, NOT PASSIVE – Often, the same questions will be asked multiple times in different ways. Be positive when answering the questions and assertive towards the answer. In an interview, I was asked, "What is one project you worked on where the business outcome was driven by cost?" I went into a description of the Citrix solution I outlined in Background and Experience in Section 2 without hesitation.

WORK THROUGH THE QUESTIONS OUT LOUD-- even if you do not know the answer. I was once asked what is a subnet with 200 IP addresses? This could easily be a question that I would get stuck on since there is a way of figuring out an exact subnet (2 (to the power of) − 2) to get the correct answer, but that math makes my brain hurt.

The interviewer did not specify which class (A, B, or C) and it confused me even more. Instead of answering "I am not sure of the answer." or something similar, I tried to figure it out. I replied, "In a class C of 192.168.1.0/24 there are 253 addressable hosts with .1 being the route and .255 being the broadcast." The interviewer is looking for exactly 200, but this gives them the idea that you at least have the basic concepts down.

Every industry has these types of questions, whether it is a specific chemical compound for a chemistry position, a drug combination that could be deadly to a customer for a pharmacist, or specific electrical voltages that gauges of wire can handle for an electrician. Whatever it is, break it down to the basics of what you do know, and outline the principals.

In-Person Interviewing

Interviewing is a skill. You must be comfortable with yourself and your capabilities. You must also be comfortable with describing and explaining those abilities not only verbally but through your body or actions.

Return to the research you have completed previously about the company, culture, and the position you are applying for. Understand your strengths in the role and understand what you will need to work on to become more proficient at it. Finally, run through a list of questions about how you would deal with a non-technical problem, for example, "How did you deal with a disagreement with a co-worker where expectations by you or him were not met. What was the outcome? How did you deal with the problem, and did it resolve the issue?"

Below is a list of tips and tricks I have learned to succeed in interviews, read through them and ask yourself if you are doing them.

SHOW UP ON TIME AND BE READY. – Phone, and video interviews or even in-person interviews, the most important piece in my mind is showing up at the right location on time and being ready to go. When the interview is in person, at a specific location, go to the location ahead of time.

Is there parking? How long will it take you to park and walk into the building? What other factors can make you late? Figure out how to mitigate the potential issues that could make you late. Do you need a friend or neighbor to take your kids to school so you can be there in plenty of time? If so, do it.

There is no room in the conversation for "Sorry I was late. I had to take my kids to school." Great, so you cannot show up on time for the most important day at the company ... the interview. What am I going to deal with later is what an interviewer is thinking.

TEST IT OUT There are several different platforms for video and voice interviews. If the interviewer is using a platform you are not familiar with, download the application, set it up and test it before the interview.

TAKE NOTES! Take a notebook with you to every interview, virtual or in person. If you miss a question or the interviewer expresses a personal belief or opinion that allows you more insight into the environment, jot it down in your notebook. At every interview, you should make at least 1 page of notes, these include every person's name who you spoke to and every question you feel could have been answered better.

AFFIRMATIVE LANGUAGE – become accustomed to using language that puts the idea in the interviewer's head you are already on the same team and working together.

"When we work together…"

"In this partnership…"

"As we continue our professional relationship…"

BE ARTICULATE. Speak in complete sentences, use industry buzz words. "Yes" is better than "yeah" or "maybe." "No" is better than "naugh." "That is interesting; let me think about it," is better than "hmmm." Remove crutch words, "like," "umm" and other similar phrases. When your interviewer is not being articulate and is speaking in a less than professional manner, keep your part of the conversation polite.

NOT KNOWING EVERYTHING IS OK. Fill in all of the detail you know of and be honest about what you do not know with phrases like "I have studied that in the past but have not worked on it recently."

Draw a correlation to a similar product or service you have used to show you understand the process.

I was once asked, "How do you troubleshoot a process that keeps crashing on start in Windows?" I clearly did not know the correct answer, or what tools should be used, however, I did know the process and could explain/demonstrate it on Mac or Linux and that was enough for the interviewer to see I understood troubleshooting at a deep level.

MAKE THE CONNECTION Eye contact and positive facial signals in a virtual setting help. I use a tip from my old boss that helps me smile and maintain positive eye contact with the people I am talking to in a virtual setting.

On, above or next to your webcam, place 1 or 2 items that make you smile and bring you joy when you look at them.

I use a $100 bill and pictures of my children, held in place by a clothespin butterfly made by my daughter. When I am looking into the camera, it is hard not to smile with those 3 things beaming down at me.

LET THE LIGHT SHINE Make sure you have plenty of light so the interviewer can see your face.

CLEAN UP Make sure the background is clean and presentable for the camera and your interviewer.

DO NOT LIE I cannot encourage this enough, do not lie. Ever. See "On Lying" in Section 2 if you need a reminder.

For in-person interviews, all the following information still holds true. Arriving on time is always number one in my book. I like to arrive about 10-15 minutes early just in case there is some last-minute change or delay I am not expecting. If for some reason, you hit every green light that day and arrive 20-30 minutes early, I'd suggest you don't wait in the parking lot like a creepy stalker. Find a nearby gas station or convenience store. Avoid the temptation to anxiously eat junk food or drink coffee, Murphy's Law guarantees you will spill on yourself out of nervousness, give yourself the 5-10 minutes of pep talk to burn time and then arrive back at the Company's office with 10-15 minutes to spare.

For one interview, I knew the location and where to park and what it would look like getting to the interview. I got out of my car and walked to the interview. As I stepped on the escalator, the heel of my dress shoe fell off. It got stuck on the escalator. It took a good 5 minutes to fish it out of the escalator and smash it back on the shoe. It was not quite right, and I walked funny, but it worked. I walked into the interview 8 minutes early and sat down and waited. The interview went well and as I walked out…. The heel came off again. It did not matter, I was on time, I was prepared for the interview, had the right answers, and let nothing deter me from making a great presentation in front of the interviewers.

GREETINGS – In today's culture, politeness and manners still have a place. When meeting someone for the first time, a few good tips to make sure you make a good impression

- Always greet the person you meet by standing up and extending your hand and saying, "Hi Mr./Mrs./Ms. [LAST NAME], my name is [Your Full Name] nice to meet you." At the time of this writing, most people are offering a quick fist bump or just a wave to avoid spreading germs, do not be offended.

- When I am introduced to someone, I like to stand up and look them in the eye while I shake their hand. I see a lot of people shake hands while they are sitting down or kind of halfway extend a hand while their attention is focused on something else. Again, a personal preference, that shows the interviewer you are a respectful professional.

ENTERING THE ROOM – Let the interviewer take the lead into the room and pick the position where they want to sit, and then when you find your chair, wait till the interviewer sits down and then take your chair.

MIRRORING – Mirroring is a technique to quickly build rapport with anyone, where you observe the interviewer's mood, actions and posture, and you as the person being interviewed closely follow suit without being obvious. If the interviewer leans in, lean in. If the interview is laid back and comfortable, do the same.

This is not only about body language but also about phrasing. When asked a difficult question that is slightly vague, you can repeat one to three words from the interviewer's question. It allows the interviewer to understand you are listening, then go into greater detail.

In an interview, you are asked, "Tell me what you know about electrical voltage?" You reply, "Electrical voltage."

The interviewer will then volunteer information that clarifies the question. "Yes, electrical voltage, like what makes up a current and how can it be measured?"

This is not foolproof. Practice it beforehand until it becomes a habit.

NOTES – As you are working through the interview, having your notebook and a pen handy is essential. Taking notes is a great way to continue to deliver value and understand the position. Keeping track of things discussed during the interview process helps when crafting your responses for follow up in the next section.

In an extremely long interview, that eventually resulted in a job offer, the interviewer asked me what I had written down.

I showed him my notebook with 9 bullet points, name of the interviewer, 2 notes about the company I had made before the interview about the company, 2 questions I had prepared ahead of time in case I got stuck. The other 3 notes were about the interview, 1 question I had flubbed, 2 more questions I was asked and answered correctly, but wanted to follow up and make sure. The bullet points simply said, "Stay cool, you got this", which I jotted down just as the interview was concluding.

The interviewer had not seen someone take notes or come as prepared as I was, and that preparation and the notes were more valuable than some of my technical shortcomings.

EXITING – At the conclusion of the interview, perform the same actions you did on entering, just in reverse. As the interviewer stands, you stand, extend your hand and say, "Thank you, Mr./Mrs./Ms. [LASTNAME] for the time to talk today, I enjoyed our discussion about [topic in the interview]. Then allow them to escort you out.

As you are walking out, listen for key information. When working as a Sales Engineer, we had a term called the "Walk Out." This is where the customer or someone in the customer's team comes clean and tells you what they thought, and what blockers or champions you have, as you are being escorted to the parking lot.

Look for some of the following indicators

- Follow on actions for you and them
- Dates they will decide by
- The interviewer's mood. Does he show you around the office before you leave or just escort you to reception?

- Does the interviewer or someone on the interview team walk you out?

Final thoughts – When you are out in your car, breathe a sigh of relief. Take out your notebook, jot down anything you did well, other items you could work on, including any you want to clarify and notes for follow up.

You completed the interview! GREAT!! Your job is not done.

Following Up

The most important consideration in following up with your interviewers is timing.

It is always a good idea to send a Thank You email, one or two days after the interview, to your point of contact and thank them for the opportunity to speak with them, and anyone else you had the chance to talk with. No matter what you think the outcome will be.

Your email should be directed to the point of contact and whomever you interviewed with. Bring up an important conversation topic you spent a few minutes on and speak to the importance of the problem the interviewer was asking about. You can ask for their feedback. This will increase your engagement with the interviewer and keep your name at the forefront of their minds. I like to make corrections here to one item I may have flubbed during the interview. Here is a quick example

"During the interview process, Joe asked me what protocol ping uses? I initially replied with TCP, and felt that was not right, I went home and researched it to make sure I was correct and found the actual protocol is ICMP."

For a copy of a <u>Thank You Letter/Email</u>

Internal recruiters are human beings just like you so thanking them for their help, no matter what it was, is an important part of making a lasting impression.

Outcome

All hiring decisions ultimately result in either an employment offer or a (hopefully polite) rejection. If the outcome is negative, meaning you were not selected for the position, it is hard to not take the decision personally but do not. In the end, someone else made a more favorable impression on the hiring manager; these things happen.

Think about it this way, you don't want to be anyone's "second best choice," waiting for an opportunity to be someone's best candidate means you'll start the job day one with an important advocate, the hiring manager who wants to show her boss she's capable of making a competent hire. Remember when I said interviewing is a skill? Well then, you have just had a good opportunity to polish your skill a bit.

If the outcome was a positive one, be gracious and wait for your paperwork. Mission accomplished.

Following up Part Deux

What to do when you have not heard back … When you have not received a response, go back to the point I made earlier, recruiters are humans and so are the hiring managers. The reason they are looking to hire you or someone like you is they are at or over capacity.

You may need to wait 1 – 2 weeks to get the results of the interview. Patience is a virtue that does not pay the rent. Try to relax and focus instead on what you will do to help the company when you get hired. Also, keep working on other contacts for other positions in other companies. Do not bet all your hopes on getting a single interview.

After two weeks, make a second follow up. It may have gotten lost in the human resources or the hiring manager's inbox or at a large company, more likely, the recruiter is actively assisting three or four managers at once and your hiring manager isn't screaming the loudest for their attention.

Reach out again with a polite and professional email reminding them you are waiting their decision. Realistically you should still be hunting for new contacts.

Yesware will flag a message that has gone without a response after one week. Use this as a reminder. Then reach out again, asking politely for an update.

If there has been no communication, file the job lead as dead in your Master List.

I Found Another Position

You are sitting there and an opportunity you've been working through the system comes in. You know the company, the hiring manager, some supporters, and contacts. AWESOME! You think.

As you are replying, another offer comes in.

What do you do?

Most people say take the highest offer; others will say you should commit to whoever replied first.

Having been in this situation before, I suggest taking a serious look at both companies and what they offer, their culture and the people you met during your in-person interview. Imagine you will be working for them for another 10 years. What can you see yourself doing at each company given the offer they gave you, and what you think the growth trajectory for that company is in the next 10 years?

Pick the best fit, not the most money. The best fit will provide you with a stable platform you can learn and build on, and the money will come in the form of your sanity and peace of mind.

Picking the most money will provide you with an initial bump in pay you can buy things with, but will it help you grow in your career? In our culture of never-ending fear of missing out and "Best Life" social media snippets from "friends" you lost touch with a decade ago designed to overstimulate your jealousy gland. It takes a mature employee to accept an offer with less direct compensation. But give the intangibles a serious thought, that job that offers $10,000 less per year? Oh, it also comes with reduced-cost health care, is only a 15-minute drive from home in rush hour traffic and gives employees half-day Fridays off every week…. trust me, those intangibles will still be providing you satisfaction long after you've nickeled and dimed your way into a higher car payment (etc.) with that extra $10,000 in salary.

Decide which company you want to work for, get all the paperwork that says you are employed in hand, and then politely decline the other offers.

Politely is the key, someone wiser than me once said, "Remember, good manners are free," you never know when you will meet that HR person or hiring manager again, and may need to work with them again to find a new position.

Negotiate or Not

In the upfront meetings with the internal recruiter where you accepted an initial offer based on the facts, you know about your skills, experience, and the position. When the recruiter comes back to ask if you accept the offer, the compensation should be in line with your initial conversation.

If the compensation offered is not in line with the position, then it is time to negotiate. I have two friends John and Matt. John and I always say, "if the offer is in line with the initial proposal, take it!" Matt says never take the first offer.

The difference that John and I have is we have both been hiring managers. Going back and reselling the candidate to human resources or whoever is a pain, but that is not really the point. What we fear as a hiring manager if you want to sit down and haggle, is when I ask you to complete a task, are you going to want to sit down and haggle more?

I have not hired a candidate new to the workforce or new to the type of role. I also make sure when I am hiring, I use an old recon moto "Yesterday was the last easy day." Explaining that we are hiring you to fill a need the company has and do not have time for discussion on matters that are clearly "See that task? Good, let me know if you have any questions but most importantly, get it done, and make sure the customer is happy with it."

John and I want to know that when we ask you something, you will give us a straight answer, and then when the task is outlined clearly, you will follow through. Haggling after agreeing on a price makes us leery that the work will come second.

Our experience has taught us that people who want to haggle over what will amount to maybe 100 or 200 extra dollars a month, will also be the same employee who will look at their job as a strict set of duties and actions they will perform along with duties they feel as though "are not in their job description." Sometimes, the candidate has returned with an embarrassingly off base counteroffer and we've rescinded our offers. If you're that out of touch with reality – you're better off working for the competition, that is, if they'll consider your "optimistic" counteroffer.

Matt has worked his entire career in account management or sales and knows that if the perception of value for what he provides is substantially higher and he knows how to articulate that value. He can list the duties he will be tasked with and then work through the list to show how he can provide value more quickly than other candidates, as well as a deeper level of understanding of what it takes to build on additional skills that will allow him to excel in the new environment he is stepping into.

Both approaches are valid. I typically urge caution when negotiating; it could mean a delay to coming off life support and preparing to run your marathon as we talked about in the first section.

If you decide to negotiate, ensure you have a bullet proof case for what you are asking for. Just saying I want 5000 $ extra a year if the offer was in your initial range you agreed to will not garner you support.

A strong case might be the cost of health care services at your new place of employment is a 50% increase over what you had paid previously. If the company is a publicly traded, and the stock which you are expecting to receive as part of your package is consistently falling, might be a reason to ask for additional compensation.

Use caution with negotiating and remember your goals of finding new employment, over a significant pay increase.

FINAL THOUGHTS

"It is what it is."

-Patricia Dobmeier Hughes

"No, mom it is what you make it."

-Erin D. Hughes

Conclusion

Finding a new position is not easy. The system laid out here is designed to help take some of the uncertainty and pain out of the process.

We covered our Mindset, giving us a bias for action and purpose. Our LinkedIn profile and Resume and Cover Letter have received an overhaul. We have covered new tools like, Yesware, Hunter IO and JobScan.co to increase our efficiency and understand where we are getting traction. Our Social Media accounts have been cleaned up.

The Master List is now our primary tool for tracking Contacts, Companies and Positions. With the workflow diagrams we can see what next steps are should be and walked through the process from applying for the contact to interviewing and accepting the offer.

We have covered finding a new position from the beginning to end. I am sure this system will help your if you follow the steps outlined here.

I would love to hear your thoughts, send me a email through the contact form here at <u>45 Days to Hired</u>

REFERENCES

How to find unemployed people on LinkedIn

Do I need a picture in my LinkedIn profile?

3 Ways to find people looking for work on LinkedIn

Talent Solutions

Social Media

Interview Buzz Words

Jobscan.co

Resume Samples at Resumes.com

Chris Voss the Black Swan Group

Never Split the Difference by Chriss Voss

Chris Voss YouTube

How to Share Public Posts on LinkedIn

The Brutal Truth

The Undercover Recruiter

LinkedIn Help Growing your network

LinkedIn Help Inviting and connecting

LinkedIn Help Build Your Professional Network

Finding People, You Know on LinkedIn--- video

Jason Stapelton-- Winners Win

MENTORS, FAMILY & FRIENDS

To all the friends, family, and co-workers, I forgot or failed to mention.

Patricia Helen Dobmeier Hughes. She taught or tried to instill in a young, impatient boy that he had to do the work. That people would always tell him he was not good enough and he would fail, but no matter what, he must keep going.

To my brother Patrick, 45 years later, when I need advice or guidance, my poor little brother is my one-stop-shop.

John Walker, for poking and prodding me along to get this "important work done" because "people out there right now need this information." Most of all, for proofreading all my horrid writing and grammar, and not falling out of your chair laughing. I will be held in no way liable for injuries related to your laughing at my poor grammar.

To my father Douglass Robert Hughes, who taught me how to swing a hammer, turn a wrench and take on problems too big for one person, like this one.

My sister Mary, achieving more through every obstacle life throws at her.

Mrs. Long, the first person outside my family who believed in me.

Don V, when you switch schools at 16 and are already socially awkward, having someone to hang out with and nudge you in the right direction is something I can never forget.

1st Sergeant Paul Jornet U.S.M.C. (RET) In 1995 I was a young wild Marine NCO. Then Staff Sergeant Jornet showed up at 4th Marines TOW PLT in Okinawa and he quickly showed me what a real leader was. Thirty plus years later, my mentor, friend, boss, and co-worker, thanks for helping me fulfill more than I ever believed I could.

Chris Tabor, I would have never had dreamed of writing this book if not for your inspiration.

Chris Lachaux, for being the best technical sounding board, friend, and mentor one could ask for.

Aunt Sue, for helping me with my family and reminding me of the power of reconnecting with your family.

Uncle Ray, for your timeless financial advice, save your money, there is always time to make more, but save your money.

Eric, to the toughest headstrong kid who is so much like his me that it pains me to see what you will have to go through to discover your own greatness.

Anna, thank you for being the thoughtful, sweet, creative young lady who I am sure will conquer the world, but first, conquer your self-doubt.

Sara, my little daredevil since birth, my little fierce fighter, keep fighting.

Epilogue

Things had not been going great at work and I was convinced I was not in "the right seat on the bus."

I thought it was time to look for a new position in a new company. A refreshing change was what I thought I needed. I looked at companies I wanted to work for and where my skills matched their needs. Following the principles outlined in this book, I reviewed connections, then at the companies they worked at. I found 2 people in my second level contacts who worked at the company I was looking to work for.

The first contact I had never directly met; we had worked for the same local Cyber Security company a few years past, he had spent a brief bit of time there immediately after I had left and I noticed from his LinkedIn profile we had similar experiences and some of the same friends.

I connected with him through LinkedIn and asked him if he had time for a call.

We spoke a couple of days later for about 30 minutes, and he filled me in on some of the special features and benefits of the company. It was a productive conversation but nothing electrifying. I agreed that I would keep in touch with him as my search progressed.

The second contact was a recruiter. She had previously worked at a local recruiting company I had used in the past to fill an open position I was hiring for in Houston. She was now a recruiter for my target company. During a brief phone call, I told her I was looking for a change and we reminisced a bit over the challenges of hiring people who were dependable. I left it at that, thinking I would need to go it on my own to get hired at this company.

A few weeks later, my company, like so many others crippled by the COVID-19 economy, initiated a reduction in force, which included my position. What else could I do? I began applying the principles in this book and working my way through my contacts.

Then seemingly out of the blue, I received a contact request from a recruiter with the company I had been trying to build my contact network in. We talked briefly, and she set me up with a technical screening. The screening went well, and I was moved on to the next phase. I was originally scheduled to have the screening in 2 weeks, but then an interview slot opened for a 5-hour screening two days later and I jumped on it. Little time to prepare, but my bias for action would not allow me to pass up this opportunity. Besides, I have always considered it important to show you can be called on at a moment's notice to solve a problem.

Bottom line, two days later, I was pleasantly shocked and humbled to receive an offer from my target employer, an impressive "A" player in my industry and a household name. I credit the speed of my transition to diligently following the processes outlined in this book. As "luck" would have it, the silver lining in all of this is that the recruiter I mentioned earlier as my second contact within the company was the contact who referred me to the recruiter who put me in the process for this new position. Often in the realm of job searching, we create our own luck by following through with old contacts even when it's uncomfortable.

While I made a few missteps along the way, sending unsolicited resumes to contacts who did not have the power to introduce me to decision-makers and filling out position-based applications. The system worked as I had designed it. Perhaps nearly as satisfying as receiving the job offer was the look on the faces of my former manager and the HR exit counselor at my last company when I politely declined the Company's offer of a paid transition counseling service because I had accepted a better position.

Ultimately the experience helped renew my faith that the system of Contacts, Companies and Positions was the correct way to go about a search for meaningful employment.

There were plenty of times I felt like bailing on the process. That the ideas I have outlined in this book would not work.

They did; my advice: build your network every damn day!

I hope the information you have learned in this book is helpful in your job search. If you are still struggling, I get a lot of requests, but I would be happy to set up a time to go over your resume, talk about your skills and what you want out of your position and help and be a part of your success.